Transforming Primary QTS

Primary English across the Curriculum

Transforming Primary QTS

Primary English
across the Curriculum

Karen Tulloch, Judith Cullen, Enid Jones,

Linda Saunders and Gillian Turner

Series editor: Alice Hansen

Los Angeles | London | New Delhi
Singapore | Washington DC

Learning Matters
An imprint of SAGE Publications Ltd
1 Oliver's Yard
55 City Road
London EC1Y 1SP

SAGE Publications Inc.
2455 Teller Road
Thousand Oaks, California 91320

SAGE Publications India Pvt Ltd
B 1/I 1 Mohan Cooperative Industrial Area
Mathura Road
New Delhi 110 044

SAGE Asia-Pacific Pte Ltd
3 Church Street
#10-04 Samsung Hub
Singapore 049483

Editor: Amy Thornton
Development Editor: Jennifer Clark
Production Controller: Chris Marke
Project Management: Deer Park Productions,
Tavistock
Marketing Manager: Catherine Slinn
Cover Design: Wendy Scott
Typeset by: PDQ Typesetting Ltd
Printed by: MPG Books Group, Bodmin, Cornwall

Library of Congress Control Number: 2012936245

British Library Cataloguing in Publication data

A catalogue record for this book is available from the
British Library

ISBN 978 0 85725 781 9
ISBN 978 0 85725 868 7 (hbk)

Contents

Acknowledgements

The authors would like to express their appreciation to Mark Cordery for his involvement in the project.

The support of colleagues and students at St Mary's University College Twickenham has been invaluable.

About the authors

Karen Tulloch

Karen has taught in several schools in London and has worked as a SENCO. She has also worked for two years in Ethiopia, moderating and managing a nationwide training programme for teacher educators. During her time there she volunteered with various NGOs and local groups teaching and supporting disadvantaged children and young people. Karen now works as a senior lecturer at St Mary's University College on the BA QTS primary programme. Her research has focused on educational psychology and currently on dyslexia.

Judith Cullen

Judith has taught in both Inner and Outer London primary schools and spent eight years as a school's Literacy Co-ordinator with responsibility for developing the school library. She now teaches as a senior lecturer on the PGCE Primary English course, contributes to undergraduate and online Masters modules at St Mary's University College and oversees PGCE Primary admissions. She has a particular interest in researching language and literacy in a wider social context and experiences of mature students.

Enid Jones

Enid has taught in a number of primary schools and also worked as an English advisory teacher for a large LEA. In her advisory role Enid was responsible for the development of English provision in the authority's schools and led working groups and classroom-based research on children's literature, reading, writing and language exploration. She has many years' experience in teacher education lecturing in English including leading a large undergraduate teacher education programme. She has co-ordinated English projects with teachers in partnerships schools including primary school library provision and shared writing and has worked as an external examiner for primary English at other universities. Her research has focused on teacher education in the teaching of reading.

Linda Saunders

Linda has had extensive teaching experience in English primary schools. She has also lectured in primary English at St Mary's University College. Linda is currently completing her doctoral studies focusing on children's reading. She has recently returned from two years studying for her PhD and teaching in New Zealand.

Gillian Turner

Gillian has taught in a number of schools in London. She has been a leading literacy teacher and organised a range of in-service workshops on poetry, storytelling and book making. Gillian has also been a deputy head teacher in a large multicultural school and has been involved in the development and mentoring for the SCITT programme in Wandsworth. She has also worked with schools to develop a whole-school initiative to improve writing. Gillian is now working as a senior lecturer at St. Mary's University on the PGCE Masters Level programme. She has written and has published a book on Shared Texts and is now writing a fiction book for children. Her research has focused on reluctant readers and improving boys' writing.

Series Editor

Alice Hansen

Alice Hansen is the Director of Children Count Ltd where she is an educational consultant. Her work includes running professional development courses and events for teachers and teacher trainers, research and publishing. Alice has worked in education in England and abroad. Prior to her current work she was a primary mathematics tutor and the programme leader for a full-time primary PGCE programme at the University of Cumbria.

Introduction

This book is one of the first in the new *Transforming Primary QTS* series, which has been established to reflect current best practice and a more creative and integrated approach to the primary school curriculum. While English is a subject that will keep a strong and discrete identity through current curriculum review, there is a clear movement within schools to approach English teaching and learning that engages and inspires children.

This book encourages you as a trainee teacher to take a critical and creative look at how you can make best use of English to support learning across the curriculum.

The importance of English should not be underestimated. Not only is it a core National Curriculum subject in its own right, it also provides children with the skills of speaking, listening, reading and writing that can be used as tools to learn all subjects.

About the book

This book takes a practical look at how you can develop children's English knowledge, skills and understanding by offering a number of opportunities to address many of the challenges of learning and teaching English in a cross-curricular way.

The book is presented in two parts. Part 1 focuses on the content of the English curriculum and how each Programme of Study can be a) taught through other curriculum subjects or b) used and applied in order to teach other subjects. You are encouraged to take a wide-ranging range of approaches to identify opportunities for developing children's English attainment.

Part 2 takes a look at some of the wider issues of using English in your wider professional role in primary education, including essential guidance on current debates and practice. You will be guided through the intricacies of using English to:

- organise learning environments, and planning;
- carry out practitioner research as a form of professional development;
- inspire and enthuse children to develop their love of English.

Learning Matters has published a number of other English-related titles. This book is complementary to these because it moves on from the core knowledge and understanding required to teach English effectively.

Using this book

Throughout this book the authors have drawn upon their extensive experience of teaching and mentoring trainee teachers to present a wide range of case studies that you can adapt and use in the classroom. The activities provided in each chapter will help you become actively engaged in strengthening your subject knowledge and developing your skills in teaching English. Each chapter concludes with a review of learning, and poses questions related to the content for you to reflect upon. Suggested responses to these self-assessment questions are included at the end of the book.

English across the curriculum

To help you find your way around this book, you can use the following tables to locate where particular subjects and themes are discussed.

Subject	Chapter	Brief description
Mathematics	2	Exploring morphology to support children's understanding of mathematical vocabulary
	3	Mathematical investigations
	4	Measures
Science	2	Using the jigsaw technique to support children's classification of the properties of materials
	4, 5	Investigating living things in their environment
ICT	4, 9	Data handling, research skills
Geography	2	Words 'borrowed' from other world languages
	9	Case studies focused on geographical knowledge
	6	Environmental changes and sustainable development
	4	Using non-fiction books to support field work
	5	Local community case study
History	2	Language change stimulated by invaders and settlers
	3	Novel set in Tudor times, case study
	5	Local community case study
	9	Broad exploration of UK case study
Music	3	Children's book case study
	5	Exploring heritage songs and rhymes, case study
	9	Topic ideas
Art and Design	2	Creating a 'three display' for the morpheme 'tri'
	3	Children's book case study
Design and Technology	5	Identifying language demands for EAL pupils
Physical Education	2, 9	Using language to describe movement
		Dance
Religious Education	2	Exploration of The Good Samaritan from different versions of the Bible
	9	Fact files of different faiths based on research
PSHE	2	Valuing and respecting all languages including standard and non-standard dialects of English
		Celebrating personal identity through the meaning and origins of names
	4	A focus on a social justice issue, citizenship
	6	Adapting to change
	5	Faith and culture in the local community, case study
	9	Citizenship
		Global issues
Drama	3, 4	Dramatising historical events

Table 1 Cross curricular issues

Issue	Chapter	Brief description
Setting up the classroom	10	Planning the layout, organisation and management of the classroom
Planning	2, 5 5, 8	Language exploration as an incidental study or a planned focus Differentiation
Assessment	7	Developing professional English for assessment
Policy Writing	7	Developing professional English for policy writing
Language Development	1 2 5 6	How children develop English capability Exploring morphology to encourage children to make connections between words Learning English as a second language Links between language and thinking
Global issues	6 9	Sustainable development Focus of chapter
Communication	2, 6 6 9 7 8	Using the jigsaw technique to support children's learning Strategies for developing talk between children Understanding of concepts Professional dialogue Developing English subject knowledge
Gender issues	4 10	Boys' reading Resourcing the classroom book corner with consideration to boys' and girls' reading preferences
Equal opportunities	2 10	Valuing and respecting all languages including standard and non-standard dialects of English Resourcing the classroom book corner for all members of the class

Table 2 Other issues

Part 1: Introduction

Part 1 of this book explores the central role of English in the primary school curriculum and in everyday life. It considers the nature of language, English in the primary curriculum, language capability and the significance of English as a core skill in a range of contexts. It explores the potential to use English across the curriculum to enhance children's learning. There is particular focus on language, literature and non-fiction texts. Consideration is also given to children learning English as an additional language who face challenges in understanding a new language and the language of each curriculum subject. Chapter 1 identifies links between language and thought and this is developed further at the end of Part 1 in an exploration of thinking skills. You are encouraged to take a creative and innovative approach to using English in a cross-curricular manner and this book supports you in doing so, by providing many practical examples of effective cross-curricular opportunities. It is hoped that you will respond to your children's interests and needs by facilitating learning which engages and educates, making links across subjects which will maximise the development of skills, knowledge and understanding. The emphasis is on providing a range of inspiring, exciting and interesting opportunities to enthuse children and to develop their learning in natural, real and stimulating ways.

1. English as a core skill

> ## Learning Outcomes
>
> This chapter aims to help you to:
> - understand the difference between English, literacy and language teaching;
> - understand more about your own use of English and language;
> - understand the development of English within the National Curriculum;
> - develop your understanding of the importance of supporting children to develop their English capability across the primary curriculum.
>
> ### TEACHERS' STANDARDS
> A teacher must:
>
> **1. Set high expectations which inspire, motivate and challenge pupils**

- establish a safe and stimulating environment for pupils, rooted in mutual respect

2. Promote good progress and outcomes by pupils

- plan teaching to build on pupils' capabilities and prior knowledge
- demonstrate knowledge and understanding of how pupils learn and how this impacts on teaching

3. Demonstrate good subject and curriculum knowledge

- have a secure knowledge of the relevant subject(s) and curriculum areas, foster and maintain pupils' interest in the subject, and address misunderstandings
- demonstrate a critical understanding of developments in the subject and curriculum areas, and promote the value of scholarship
- demonstrate an understanding of and take responsibility for promoting high standards of literacy, articulacy and the correct use of standard English, whatever the teacher's specialist subject

Introduction

This chapter introduces a key premise of this book: that English is a core skill; proficiency enables us to interact, learn and to function in many different areas of life. The skill of using English can be applied to different circumstances and different curricular areas and can be considered a 'core skill' as it is highly useful in our everyday lives. For the purpose of this chapter, a skill is considered as something that is applied and develops through practice. This chapter is designed to pinpoint key areas in the use of English across the curriculum that are fully developed in the remainder of this book. The chapter begins by addressing the question of English capability in the light of a brief outline of the developmental process of language.

Using English in the world around us

Some adults and children believe that the core English skills of reading and writing are confined to the classroom and that once acquired do not play a significant part in the daily world. In addition there is the tacit assumption that the underlying skills of speaking and listening, that are core parts of English in the National Curriculum, do not need attention because they develop of their own accord.

Activity

To help you to think about English as a core skill, look at the list of everyday tasks. Choose one task and list the reading, writing, speaking and listening skills necessary to achieve it. This is designed to help you to consider how a number of everyday tasks require a range of different reading, writing, speaking and listening skills

Writing an email to the bank	Reading a tax return	Speaking to the GP at the surgery	Deciding who to vote for in a general election
Doing the weekly shop	Choosing a book to read for pleasure in the local library	Planning a holiday	Writing a love letter
Cooking a new recipe	Surfing the Internet for the most fuel-efficient car	Negotiating with the prospective buyer of your house	Making a speech at a family wedding

How did you manage the activity? Even everyday tasks like speaking to the GP at the surgery will require a range of English skills. For example:

- reading the calendar to fix an appointment date;
- preparing for the consultation by writing down your list of symptoms;
- choosing the appropriate language if you are bilingual;
- speaking clearly to the GP so that he or she can make a rapid and accurate diagnosis;
- listening to the GP's medical advice and asking appropriate questions if necessary;
- locating the chemist with the prescription and reading the instructions for its administration;
- repeating the process if symptoms persist.

Tasks analysing the necessary English skills in this way allows you to see the central place of English in everyday life and perhaps to what extent such skills are taken for granted by those who are competent users. It cannot be argued that these tasks could be completed independently without the applied use of English skills. However an individual's response as to what skills are necessary for each may be influenced by personal responses to English that are largely intuitive. Many of these intuitive responses are based on what individuals perceive as the nature, purpose and context of English in life. Such notions are closely linked to a clear judgement and understanding of the constituents of effective English skills for lifelong use. This includes English for recreational, academic and social uses.

Research Focus: The development of English within the National Curriculum

In the lead-up to the creation of the first National Curriculum for English the Cox Report, published in 1988, recognised the breadth of English. Five possible 'views' or models of English were identified in the Cox Report.

A 'personal growth' view was identified as one which should help children to grow personally. Through literature, discussion and imaginative writing children are enabled to come to a deeper understanding of themselves and others. They develop their imagination and their interpersonal and communication skills.

→

A 'cross-curricular' view, particularly relevant to the topic of this book, identifies that English should enable children to cope with the demands of learning across the school curriculum. It recognises that children learn English for other subjects and that they also learn about English in other subjects.

In keeping with the 'functional' view of literacy, an 'adult needs' view stresses that English should enable children, ultimately, to cope with the oracy and literacy demands of the adult world.

A 'cultural heritage' view places importance on introducing children to 'our' literary cultural heritage, to the 'best' poetry, novels and plays that have been written in the language.

Finally, in a 'cultural analysis' view, which aligns with a critical view of literacy, children are taught to interpret and question and to 'read against the text.' (Cox 1989 2.20) The report asserted that these views are not the only possible views and they are not sharply distinguishable or mutually exclusive. Nonetheless, they do offer a broad basis for consideration of priorities within the English curriculum.

Activity

Take a few minutes to consider the five views of English teaching outlined above.

Is it possible to place them in an order of importance?

What are 'the best' examples of literature in the language?

Whose heritage is referred to in 'our'?

Which view(s) of English is/are closest to your priorities for English teaching?

Table 1.1 on page 8 outlines each of the five views of English teaching and provides examples of how each might be explored using a cross-curricular approach in the classroom.

The first National Curriculum for English and the National Literacy Strategy

The National Curriculum for English was published in 1990 (DES, 1990). The curriculum was informed in part by national projects in oracy and writing that had evolved during the 1980s drawing on the work of practising teachers. It set out three 'Programmes of Study': Speaking and Listening, Reading and Writing and five 'Attainment Targets': Speaking and Listening, Reading, Writing, Spelling and Handwriting. These modes were inter-related. Similarly, cross-curricular learning is an excellent vehicle for linking English and other subjects. Attainment Targets in English can be effectively achieved through, for example, history topics or PSHE work.

View of English	Activities	Texts and other resources
Personal Growth	A Year 6 child is placed in the 'hot seat' to answer questions about how s/he might have responded to being evacuated to a strange household during World War II.	The novel *Goodnight Mister Tom* by Michelle Magorian. *Goodnight Mister Tom* DVD.
Cross-curricular	A group of Year 1 children report back verbally on their science investigation on sorting and using materials before contributing to a whole class report in shared writing.	Agreed classroom rules on speaking and listening. Experience and models of 'report' texts. Whiteboard or interactive whiteboard for teacher modelling.
Adult Needs	A Year 5 child exploring the Victorians produces estate agent 'blurbs' to sell a large Victorian town house and a mill worker's terraced cottage.	Examples of estate agent house details online and/or from local agents. Children would need to have explored features of these 'adult world' texts in English before trying out their own 'sales pitch' in history.
Cultural Heritage	Children in Year 2 discuss and compare story themes.	*The Story Tree*, Hugh Lupton. *Lila and the Secret of Rain*, David Conway. *The Princess and the White Bear King*, Tanya Roby Batt.
Cultural Analysis	A Year 4 class explore bias and persuasion in writing using alternative versions of familiar stories as their starting point. (PSHE)	*The True Story of the Three Little Pigs* by Jon Scieszka and Lane Smith. *The Tough Princess* by Martin Waddell and Patrick Benson. *The Three Little Wolves and the Big Bad Pig* by Eugenios Trivizas and Helen Oxenbury.

Table 1.1 The five views of English teaching

The work of Graves (1981; 1983) was very influential in exploring the writing process rather than just the product of writing. This included drafting and editing according to purpose, audience and context and Smith (1982) linked the skills of composition and transcription to the contrast between the work of 'author' and 'secretary'. In the 1995 review of the National Curriculum the assessment criteria for spelling and handwriting were amalgamated with those for writing, combining the compositional and transcriptional dimensions of writing in one attainment target. This structure of three programmes of study and three attainment targets was maintained in the 2000 review of the curriculum although the National Literacy Strategy (NLS), which had set out a termly framework from Reception to Year 6 in 1998 (DfEE, 1998), only identified objectives for reading and writing. The National Curriculum placed emphasis on children's exposure to a range and variety of texts and the National Literacy Strategy also placed emphasis on different genres of writing. Cross-curricular learning can provide excellent contexts for exploration of these different genres.

The revised framework for English

In the revised framework the Primary National Strategy (DCSF, 2006) identified twelve strands across speaking, listening, drama, reading and writing and set out fiction, non-fiction and poetry blocks as the core content for curriculum planning. The revised framework aimed to provide a clearer picture of progression across the primary years. The framework also drew on the Rose Report on *The Teaching of Early Reading* (DCSF, 2006) and the work of Gough and Tumner (1986) in setting out a 'simple view of reading' which identified language comprehension processes and word recognition processes as children move from learning to read to reading to learn. Cross-curricular contexts can be particularly significant for the application of developing reading skills and this will be explored further in Chapters 3 and 4.

What is English capability?

English capability involves the ability both to use and reflect on language in a wide range of contexts within the four language modes of speaking, listening, reading and writing. The range of ability is sometimes referred to as a language 'repertoire'. Concepts of what counts as literacy are constantly changing. At the beginning of the twentieth century if a person could sign their own name on the marriage register rather than putting an 'X' by someone else's writing, they were deemed to be literate. Today studies such as those conducted by the Organisation for Economic and Cooperative Development (OECD, www.oecd.org) and Progress in International Reading Literacy Study (PIRLS, www.nfer.ac.uk/pirls) enable us to compare literacy data from across the world. Clearly the ability to write a name on a register would no longer be a measure of functional literacy.

Children have to develop their language repertoire and to be able to make appropriate choices according to purpose, context and audience. Whilst the necessary skills may be taught in English lessons, cross-curricular contexts provide a valuable opportunity for children to develop and apply what they have learned (Barnes, 2009). Speaking and listening generally occur in shared contexts. In contrast reading and writing allow us to communicate over time and space. These contexts influence the nature of how we use and apply the different modes of language. Speakers' resources are influenced by a shared physical environment, the human voice and body and the co-operative, interpersonal nature of speech. This enables the speaker to draw on intonation, volume, gesture and body language. The listener can ask for more detail or for instant clarification of any misunderstandings and can also cooperate and encourage the speaker.

Most children enter school with well-developed skills in spoken language. Ask any parents of four or five year olds and they will probably be able to describe a child who is very accomplished, for example, in the genre of verbal persuasion! As you will read in the next section of this chapter, many preschool children also know a good deal about written language but communicating in a reader-writer context places different demands on the participants and this should not be underestimated in a child's journey to becoming a reader and writer. A cross-curricular approach to learning can enable a variety of opportunities and contexts for children to develop both reading and writing. The different purposes afforded by using this approach are of great benefit in that children can gain experience of writing for different audiences and in different contexts.

Not all written texts are formal of course and some spoken texts, such as political speeches, are actually pre-prepared written text that is read aloud. Both spoken and written language operate on a continuum of formality and children have to develop their ability to make appropriate choices for the context, audience and purpose of their communication.

What might this look like in the case of a Year 6 child? The following case study describes the achievement in English and in the application of English skills in other curriculum subjects from two Year 6 end of year reports to parents. While you are reading the reports, think about what they are telling you about the child's achievement in English and the evidence for this. Think also about the cross-curricular links and how English is used as a core skill across the curriculum.

Case Study: Year 6 school reports

Report one is about Barry, a Year 6 boy beyond the standards required at the end of Key Stage 2. Report two is about Georgina, a Year 6 girl achieving within the required standards.

English

Barry has provided interesting and valuable contributions to our literacy discussions. He works well in paired and small group tasks. During our speaking and listening activities, including a radio broadcast and debate, Barry worked well in his group but remained quiet when communicating to the audience. He has an excellent understanding of a range of texts and is able to provide a logical opinion about a piece of writing answering questions which are only implied from the passage.

Barry is able to think about the purpose of his writing and adapt the style and tone accordingly. He varies his sentence structure so that it is more interesting for the reader and has a large repertoire of punctuation skills. During our work on Michael Morpugo Barry produced an excellent booklet detailing the plot and key character studies. Class work is presented carefully and demonstrates a good awareness of spelling conventions. Barry is currently working just above the expected level for his year group.

Geography

Barry showed real enthusiasm for the rainforest topic and produced an outstanding topic book, with a mixture of exciting information and interesting artwork. His research skills were excellent; he used the information gathered from a wide range of sources in an imaginative, creative manner. I am amazed by the sheer quantity of work that he was able to produce on such a wide range of themes. He participated keenly in discussions, displaying a thorough understanding of sustainability issues. Barry is enjoying the current geography topic on our school journey to Purbeck and is producing a pleasing book, full of neat, accurate maps. Some excellent skills are being developed. This has been a truly amazing term's work – well done!

$\rightarrow$

English

I have been really pleased by Georgina's attitude, both in class and at home; she is always so eager to complete work to the very best of her ability and has made excellent progress. She is attentive in oral activities, listening to others' ideas and opinions and is willing to offer her own contributions. In class, Georgina is eager to read aloud showing fluency. She displays a good understanding of the texts we read and an increased ability to infer meaning. Georgina is able to write for a variety of audiences and purpose. Her Macbeth booklet was fantastic, with the storyboard, letter and character study all really well developed. She displays a keen interest in all of her written work but particularly enjoyed the 'spy mission'. She organised and structured this piece of work really well, using a range of sentence types, a variety of connectives, well chosen vocabulary and with a strong storyline and interesting characterisation. Georgina tries really hard on her spellings each week and achieves well in tests. This is a target area for future development for Georgina as she does struggle with the application of letter sounds when concentrating on her writing composition. She is working at the expected level for her year group.

History

Georgina has a keen interest in history and worked steadily on the Victorian topic, producing a pleasing book. Great improvements were made in her ability to select material appropriately. She became even more motivated with the World War Two topic, developing an excellent understanding of this period of time. She worked quickly and efficiently, displaying excellent research skills by obtaining information from a variety of sources. Her topic book was comprehensive, with an interesting balance of thoroughly written accounts and pictures.

Barry and Georgina have achieved secure skills in English and demonstrated that they can use these skills in other areas of learning. Children will need a confident ability in speaking, listening, reading and writing to meet the demands of the secondary school curriculum and it is important that they have had the chance to develop and apply these skills across the curriculum during their years in primary school.

How do children develop English capability?

Children's initial experiences of using language to communicate are likely to be through the medium of spoken language. There is a real purpose for children to learn to speak; they are not learning English in isolation but in order to communicate. Thus speaking is a tool and used for a reason; for example to gain attention. Similarly, listening, reading and writing are also most effectively developed when purpose is paramount. Children develop English capability when there is motivation to do so. It is judicious to ensure that children's learning has purpose and that audience and communication are central to their development of skills and knowledge in English.

It is important to note that developing language is a recursive rather than linear process. Children need to revisit what they have learned and will repeat and relearn often. They will build on what they know, but also need opportunities to revisit and repeat what they have learned. Children's learning is influenced by experience and links to other learning. This is considered a strong argument for a cross-curricular approach to learning. It is not necessary, or even possible, to move sequentially through specific steps in order to move through progressive 'stages' of language learning. Capability in English does not result from a sequence of steps worked through in a linear fashion. It is developed as experiences and knowledge affect other experiences and knowledge and build on learning.

It is imperative that you recognise and value the vast and rich experience of language that children bring with them to the classroom. Neglecting to do so could be potentially frustrating or confusing for children starting school, as well as inhibiting optimum learning. Before they start school, children have been tremendously exposed to and engaged with language. They are immersed in language in the home and it is this experience which contributes first to children's capability in English. It is this indispensable foundation which you must then build on by creating and providing a rich and varied experience of language learning for children in school. Cross-curricular learning enables beneficial links to be made for children to learn in a natural and advantageous way. Language learning is not compartmentalised and should not be made artificially so by a restrictive curriculum or approach. Language learning occurs best in an environment rich with variety, stimuli, diversity and opportunity.

It is critical to remember Cox's assertion that 'Reading is much more than the decoding of black marks upon the page: it is a quest for meaning and one which requires the reader to be an active participant' (DES, 1989 p16.2) and to apply this principle to all four modes of language. It is crucial that children's attempts to speak, read and write are encouraged and that necessary skills are developed in a natural, enjoyable way.

Research Focus

There is much debate about how children acquire language and how they learn to use it. No single theory explains everything, but several seminal theories inform our understanding and are important to consider.

One theory of language acquisition is that language is learned through models of language. Skinner (1957) posited a behaviourist point of view that children learn language through external stimuli. This suggests that children imitate spoken language.

Although children do learn language through imitation, this does not entirely explain children's ability to generate sentences they have never heard before. Structural linguist Chomsky (1957) rejected the view that children learn entirely in response to stimuli. He argued that children are born with a capacity for language. Indeed, Chomsky asserted that children are born with knowledge of structures of language. This innate knowledge is developed through experience, which enables children to learn new vocabulary and become increasingly proficient in using language. The propensity to learn language, Chomsky argued, is in-built.

$\rightarrow$

Chomsky revolutionised views on language acquisition with his assertion that children do not simply imitate, but are equipped with a cognitive device to understand and manipulate the complexity of language. Chomsky popularised the idea of humans possessing a 'Language Acquisition Device' which exists alongside a 'Language Assistance System' (Chomsky, 1957), both present in children and working in unison to enable language development.

Russian psychologist Vygostky shared Piaget's perception of children as active learners. Piaget (1926) and Vygotsky (1978) both professed the importance of play as a method of learning and placed emphasis on the role of language within this. Crucially, Vygostky's belief was that children made sense of their world through their interactions with more experienced others and through the use of cultural tools, one of which is language. Vygotsky described the gap between a child's performance and a child's potential as the Zone of Proximal Development (Vygotsky,1978). The significance of this to children's language acquisition lies in the opportunities they are afforded, the models around them and the support they are provided. Bruner developed the concept of scaffolding learning (Bruner, 1960) which, in the context of language development, could include supporting and encouraging a child and designing activities to facilitate small, manageable steps to be taken in developing language capability.

Extending English capability in the primary school

The wealth of preschool experience is of great value to the child and also to the teacher. This section takes the richness of language already known to the child as a starting point for the teacher; a strong and exciting foundation to be built upon and enhanced. For children's capability in English to be extended, the experience they have already had (and continue to have alongside their school experience) must be nurtured, valued and celebrated. It is also worth noting that there is variance between children's experience at home and the related expertise with which they start school. For many reasons, children are not always immersed in optimal opportunities to develop language. It is incumbent on you to be aware of and develop children's experiences accordingly, recognising needs and personalising learning in order to maximise opportunity and progress.

The diversity of experience prior to starting school enhances its richness. Of pivotal importance is how this diversity is recognised, responded to and celebrated. Children must know that *their* language is valued. Many children will have experience of other languages and for many English will not be the first language of the home. Also, many different forms of English are spoken in the home. Respect for and understanding of these forms is crucial and this will be further explored in Chapter 2.

Language in different contexts

When children come to school they may find that the language of the school is significantly different from that of the home. This can be apparent as children may use a form of non-standard English at home or speak a language other than English. However, it can also be more subtle. New vocabulary may have to be learned and previously unheard phrases or instructions deciphered. Clarity and sensitivity are required to support children in adjusting to the language of the school.

Activity

Consider your journey home today and your subsequent arrival at home. Try to list in the table below all the examples of language (English or other) that you came across. There may be some overlap between columns, but the columns will help you to think about the different modes of language around us. Some examples are included as suggestions.

Language you saw/ read (print)	Language you heard	Language you created (spoken)	Language you created (written)
Bus stop signs Newspaper Shop names	Lyrics to a song on the radio TV programme People chatting on the bus	Phone call to friend Thanking bus driver	Text message to friend Shopping list

Were you surprised by the extent to which you use language in your daily life? Was the language you observed in different forms? (e.g. some may have been formal and others more colloquial, some may have been to advertise and others to inform). Does this richness of language experience exist also for young children?

Consider the range of opportunities for and instances when children might use language in their daily lives. Fill in the same table as above from the perspective of a child. Would there be differences? What would these be?

Children's English capability develops through experience. This experience provides building blocks for children to develop expertise and proficiency. Language use occurs naturally, but teachers should aim to maximise this and to provide rich, varied, stimulating and purposeful opportunities for children to develop English capability. Responding positively and encouraging children to experiment, take risks and play with language will enhance their language development. Facilitating exploration of language and celebration of its richness and diversity will further create the optimum conditions for children to develop capability. It is crucial that children are valued as a rich resource of language and that abundant opportunities across the curriculum are enabled within a stimulating environment which celebrates the many forms of language.

Recognising English in all subjects ,

The preceding exploration of language and English in the National Curriculum has focused on English as a discrete National Curriculum subject. Indeed, the Expert Panel's report for the National Curriculum review (DfE, 2011) recommended that the new National Curriculum should retain discrete and focused elements within the Programme of Study for English, and introduce statements about oral language and its development into each Programme of Study for all core and foundation subjects.

However, most National Curriculum subjects will have many links to literacy with numerous opportunities for language and literacy skills to be employed and developed. It is important to consider carefully all four modes when making decisions about how to realise opportunities for developing children's literacy skills and knowledge together with specific understanding in other curriculum areas. This could be, for example, oral debating on a topical geographical issue, classifying scientific information into labelled charts or tables, reading worded multiplication problems in mathematics, writing a diary entry from a historical character's perspective or creating an interactive, hyperlinked electronic text. If the links that teachers are able to make are creative and engaging for pupils, their learning will be deep, enhanced and highly developed (Barnes, 2009).

How do teachers explicitly draw out English skills across the curriculum?

The word 'curriculum' has its origin in Latin and can be translated as 'to run a course'. It is important, therefore, to carefully consider how primary schools organise their overall curriculum as there are a number of different 'courses' or models that they may choose to use.

The choice of curriculum that a school makes is usually in response to the particular school context, expectations of the wider community and specific student needs. It will also be influenced, in part, by government policy. The National Curriculum from 2014 will be a minimum statutory entitlement for children and schools will have the flexibility and freedom to design a wider school curriculum to meet the needs of their pupils and decide how to teach it most effectively (DfE, 2011).

Activity

Consider your own primary school education and recent placements. What curriculum model(s) did the schools follow?

Were individual subjects – mathematics, history, science etc - timetabled rigidly and taught discretely? Perhaps, instead, the children studied a range of topics, for example, *Toys* in Key Stage 1 or *The Victorians* in Key Stage 2, which had a main focus on design and technology or history but also incorporated aspects from other subjects such as art, geography and music. Did the school advance children's learning through an 'integrated day' approach, where there were no clear distinctions between areas of learning? It may be that you gained experience of other curriculum models, if so, why they may have been used?

If you experienced subject specific sessions – perhaps a daily literacy lesson where children were taught the skills of speaking, listening, reading and writing – and discrete lessons in other curriculum areas where literacy skills were not mentioned or addressed, the model under consideration would be that of content-driven, separate subject coverage which is currently more prevalent within the secondary education sector. This model has its origins – or perceived origins – in very early universal education based on the ideas of 'forms' of knowledge and university subject 'disciplines' (Kerry, 2010) and the late nineteenth/early twentieth century utilitarian elementary education models and it remains a central construct in National Curriculum development in England.

A themed approach to teaching and learning combines diverse subjects within, and across, teaching sessions. In some schools *topics* are carried out over a sustained period of time, lasting between one week and a term. Most cross-curricular approaches are designed to offer children the opportunity to work in greater depth than a subject-specific approach and can be effectively planned while meeting the statutory requirements of a subject-focused national curriculum. This is achieved by giving children more time to consolidate skills and knowledge and transfer their learning through a range of school experiences. Incorporated into this model could be opportunities for children to gain higher order thinking skills (which are explored further in Chapter 6) where they consider what they are learning and thinking which Flavell (1979) termed 'metacognition'.

Children do not learn in a linear fashion. This has implications for the primary classroom as most children do not immediately understand taught concepts, gain knowledge or develop skills at initial exposure. An example of this, that you may have already come across, would be those children who are able to correctly learn words for a weekly spelling test but are then unable to spell the same words correctly in their independent writing just a few days later. This may occur for a number of reasons. The art of writing involves both compositional and transcriptional elements and over-concentration on certain elements of the writing process means that others – in this instance spelling – get overlooked. A child may also not have understood fully the links between the words in their spelling list and word meanings or they have had insufficient time to recognise the ways in which to approach a particular spelling and have only placed that spelling into their short term memory.

Therefore it is important that you explore and recognise the difference between *shallow* and *deep* learning, the former being a superficial grasp of a skill or concept, while the latter involves developing clear cognition. While shallow learning can be seen as remembering, deep learning is *understanding* what has been remembered. Cross-curricular models will, by their explicit focus on over-learning and metacognition, lend themselves to addressing the depth of understanding necessary for effective learning.

How can English skills be embedded within the curriculum?

The teaching and learning of literacy across the curriculum should have distinct aims. Wray has expressed these as allowing children to broaden and practise their acquired literacy skills in a range of contexts and media, develop their understanding of subject-specific ways of communicating, debating and developing and also to enhance the learning in other subjects and children's motivation towards learning in those subjects (Wray, 2006).

Primary school teachers are expected to teach most National Curriculum subjects over the period of an academic year. While it is unlikely you are training as a subject specialist, your training will encompass theoretical overviews and practical teaching experience in most subjects. This should give you a secure grounding in the subject specific skills and knowledge that primary aged pupils children need to acquire. You will have the benefit of being in the position of being able to constantly reinforce core English skills through the range of other curriculum subjects. This should enable you to make reference to over-arching themes and ideas as well as being able to focus in on individual children's strengths and areas for improvement when planning and teaching. The following case study will illustrate this.

Case Study: The creative curriculum

Helen is a PGCE student who has just embarked on her second and final school placement in an inner city primary school. Working within a three-form entry school where teachers hold weekly after school meetings to plan the following week's lessons, Helen was asked for her input into the forthcoming half term topic of 'Growing' for Year 3 classes. The school followed a cross-curricular approach which would involve a visit to a local ecology centre as well as sessions in the school's outdoor areas. In terms of literacy, the class teachers were keen to incorporate the children's developing knowledge of organisational devices within non-chronological report texts as well as their ability to create their own reports using a range of planning techniques into the weekly plans.

Helen considered the progression expected of most Year 3 children. She gave considerable thought to the grammatical aspects of reading and writing such as time, cause and effect subordinating conjunctions, present tense writing and the use of commas for lists which could be developed throughout the topic. Further emphasis was also given to the use of ICT as it was expected that considerable collection of data and graph creation would take place as would developing children's mathematical understanding of different units of measure. Helen's research into the skills and knowledge that she would be expected to develop in the children in her placement class enabled her to attend the planning meeting with confidence and a keenness to share some creative ideas which could be incorporated into the planned visits and sessions.

Links to the National Curriculum

Helen became familiar with the National Curriculum's Science programme of study for KS2. She explored 'Life processes and living things', which included aspects of human and animal growth as well as conditions for healthy development of plants. Helen also focused on identifying scientific investigative skills as she was aware that fair testing, detailed, systematic observations and measurements of plants would need to be undertaken by the children. Links with Mathematics and Information and Communication Technology would support the communication and presentation of data needed throughout the topic. In terms of literacy development, it was important for Helen to explore the NC links to reading for information as well as the writing strand for composition, planning and drafting and language structure. She also found it useful to refer to Strands 9 and 10 of the PNS Framework for Literacy in respect of shaping and organising texts and strand 11 for linked aspects of grammatical writing to ensure that she was clear about age appropriate expectations.

Learning Outcomes Review

This chapter began by describing the essential place of English in everyday activities. The intuitive nature of this reading, writing, speaking and listening, for the skilled user of English, can preclude their identification. This can inhibit adequate teaching of English across the primary curriculum. By developing a personal perspective of the nature, purpose and context for English usage, you can begin to identify cross-curricular opportunities. Such opportunities will necessarily incorporate consideration of the nature of effective English skills and how to assess them.

The remainder of the chapter outlined the contexts for cross-curricular English teaching that underlie the chapters in the book that follow. First, an overview of the historical development of the national curriculum provided insight into the political and pedagogical research that has influenced the current status of primary English teaching in England and Wales. Second, the fundamental status of speaking and listening alongside reading and writing was reviewed. Finally cross-curricular approaches to primary English were examined alongside current models of curriculum delivery.

Self-assessment questions

1. Why do you think primary English skills, knowledge or understanding are often not overtly addressed in all curriculum areas?
2. Identify five reading, writing, speaking and listening skills you have used in the last 24 hours.

3. How far would a change in the intended audience or context for these five examples alter your use of them?

Further Reading

Copping, A. (2011) Curriculum approaches. In Hansen, A. (ed) (2011) *Transforming QTS Primary Professional Studies*. Exeter: Learning Matters Ltd., pp23–43.
In this chapter, Adrian Copping discusses how a cross-curricular approach to learning and teaching can deepen learning through the joining of concepts and ideas.

DfE (2011) The framework for the national curriculum. A report by the expert panel for the national curriculum review. London: DfE.
This provides a justification of the recommended approach for the 2014 National Curriculum.

References

Alexander, R. et al. (2009) *Children, their World, their Education. Final Report and Recommendations of the Cambridge Primary Review*. Oxford: Routledge.

Barnes, J. (2009) www.music-ite.org.uk/resources/primary-ite/teaching-music-cross-curricular-contexts

Bruner, J. (1960) *The Process of Education*. Cambridge, Mass: Harvard University Press.

Chomsky, N. (1957; 1965) *Syntactic Structures*. Berlin: Mouton.

DCSF (2006) *Independent Review of the Teaching of Early Reading (Rose Review)*. London: UK HMSO.

DCSF (2006) The Primary National Strategies http://nationalstrategies.standards.dcsf.gov.uk

DCSF (2009) *Independent Review of the Primary Curriculum: Final Report (Rose Review)*. Nottingham: HMSO.

DES (1988; 1989) *Cox Report: the Report of the National Curriculum. English Working Group*. London: DES.

DES (1989) *English for ages 5 to 16: Proposals of the Secretary of State for Education and Science and the Secretary of State for Wales*. UK: HMSO.

DES (1990) *English in the National Curriculum (no. 2)*. UK: HMSO.

DfE (2011) *The framework for the national curriculum. A report by the Expert Panel for the National Curriculum review*. London: DfE.

DfEE (1998) *The National Literacy Strategy: Framework for Teaching*. The Stationery Office.

DfEE (1999) *The National Curriculum Handbook for Primary Teachers in England in key stages 1 and 2*. London: The Stationery Office.

DfES (2003) *Every Child Matters: Change for Children in Schools*. London: DfES. Available at www.dcfs.gov.uk/everychildmatters/about/aims/outcomes/

DFES (2003) Excellence and Enjoyment. Available at www.dfes.gov.uk/primarydocument

DFES (2003) *Primary National Strategy. Speaking, Listening, Learning: working with children in Key Stages 1 and 2 Handbook*. DFES Norwich: HMSO.

DfES (2007) *The Early Years Foundation Stage: Setting the Standards for Learning, Development and Care for children from birth to five*. Nottingham: DfES.

Flavell, J.H. (1979) Metacognition and cognitive monitoring: A new area of cognitive-developmental inquiry. *American Psychologist, 34*, 906–911.

Gillard, D. (2010) Education in England: A brief history. Available at: www.educationengland.org.uk/history

Gough, P.B. and Tumner, W.E. (1986) Decoding Reading and Reading Disability. *Remedial Special Education*, 7: 6–10.

Graves, D. (1983) *Writing: Teachers and Children at Work*. USA: Heinemann Educational Books.

Kerry, T. (ed) (2010) *Cross-Curricular Teaching in the Primary School: Planning and Facilitating Imaginative Lessons*. Routledge.

Kingman, J. (1988) *The Kingman Report. Report of the Committee of Inquiry into the Teaching of English Language*. London: HMSO. Available at:www.educationengland.org.uk/documents/ kingman/kingman00.html

Martin, J.R., Christie, F. and Rothery, J. (1987) Social Processes in education: a reply to Sawyer and Watson (and others). In Reid, I. (ed) *The Place of Genre in Learning*.

OECD www.oecd.org

Piaget, J. (1926) *The Language and Thought of the Child*. UK: Kegan, Paul, Trench, Trubner & Co.

PIRLS www.nfer.ac.uk/pirls

Plowden, B. (1967) *The Plowden Report. Children and their Primary Schools*. London: HMSO. Available at: www.educationengland.org.uk/documents/plowden

QCDA (1997) The National Curriculum for KS1 & KS2. http://curriculum.qcda.gov.uk

Skinner, B.F. (1957) *Verbal Behavior*. Acton, MA: Copley Publishing Group.

Smith, F. (1982) *Writing and the Writer*. Great Britain: Heinemann Educational Books.

Vygotsky, L.S. (1978) *Mind and society: The development of higher mental processes*. Cambridge, MA: Harvard University Press.

Wray, D. (2006) *Teaching Literacy Across the Primary Curriculum*. Exeter: Learning Matters.

2. Language

4. Plan and teach well structured lessons

- impart knowledge and develop understanding through effective use of lesson time
- promote a love of learning and children's intellectual curiosity
- set homework and plan other out-of-class activities to consolidate and extend the knowledge and understanding pupils have acquired
- reflect systematically on the effectiveness of lessons and approaches to teaching
- contribute to the design and provision of an engaging curriculum within the relevant subject area(s)

5. Adapt teaching to respond to the strengths and needs of all pupils

- know when and how to differentiate appropriately, using approaches which enable pupils to be taught effectively
- have a secure understanding of how a range of factors can inhibit pupils' ability to learn, and how best to overcome these
- demonstrate an awareness of the physical, social and intellectual development of children, and know how to adapt teaching to support pupils' education at different stages of development
- have a clear understanding of the needs of all pupils, including those with special educational needs; those of high ability; those with English as an additional language; those with disabilities; and be able to use and evaluate distinctive teaching approaches to engage and support them

6. Fulfil wider professional responsibilities

- develop effective professional relationships with colleagues, knowing how and when to draw on advice and specialist support
- deploy support staff effectively

Introduction

Capacity for language is innate and is what sets us apart from all other creatures on the planet. Without language the world as we know it would not have evolved, and the world in our classrooms provides an excellent cross-curricular context for children to further their language development.

This chapter explores more about the unique nature of language; how the language of English has evolved and continues to change and the different ways in which other subjects can both enhance children's language use and benefit from a language focus. You may also want to consider that, for many children, English may not be their first language but that many of the principles of enhancing language ability and enhancing learning will still be highly applicable as these children reflect on their own first language across the curriculum. You will read more about children learning English as an additional language in Chapter 5.

Why is language so important across the curriculum?

Language has four modes: speaking, listening, reading and writing. All four modes are fundamental to children's personal development and educational progress. Children learn through language, they also learn to use language and they learn about language as they reflect on their own language use and that of others. Concepts in other subjects can be enhanced and consolidated through a focus on language and language capacity can be developed in interactive contexts in other subjects.

Learning through language

Once children learn to speak, language is their primary strategy for learning about themselves and the world around them. Before acquiring language children will explore the world through observation and physically, often by putting objects in their mouths. By school age the skills of observation and physical handling of objects will continue to be very important but consideration of how many times in a day young children ask the question 'Why?' is illustration of the significance of language in their growing understanding of the world.

Research Focus

During the second half of the twentieth century there was considerable research that has contributed greatly to our understanding of how children learn through language. Much of this research has shaped the classroom practice we recognise today and some has been significant in national educational policy development.

Piaget saw children as active learners. His developmental stage theory identified the progression of children's reasoning with reference to egocentrism (Piaget, 1926). By contrast Vygotsky, who was writing in the 1920s and 1930s and translated for the west in the 1970s and 1980s, saw children as social beings. He placed emphasis on children's interactions with others, particularly more experienced others. Vygotsky described language as one of the 'cultural tools' with which children interact with others and learn about the world around them (Vygotsky, 1986). Importantly, through discussion and reading, language also enables children to learn about the world beyond their immediate experience. Vygotsky's notion of the 'zone of proximal development' and Bruner's recognition of how 'scaffolding' limits the complexity of tasks, perhaps by reducing possibilities, led to an increased awareness of children's learning through language in supportive contexts (Bruner, 1960). Halliday's notion of 'learning how to mean' identified that children arrive in school with language as a means for learning (Halliday, 1975) and Wells' research of language use in the home identified the need for classrooms to develop the home like strategies of 'guidance and contingent responsiveness'

$\longrightarrow$

(Wells, 1986). Talk came to be recognised as the crucial factor which enables children to relate new knowledge to existing understanding as they internalise external knowledge and move towards conscious control. All this resulted in a focus on learning rather than teaching and children's talk, rather than teacher talk, was increasingly emphasised in classrooms. More recently de Bono's (1970) exploration into thinking further enhanced the place of language in learning.

Not all the research, however, had positive outcomes for language and learning. Bernstein's identification of 'elaborated' and 'restricted' codes of language was misinterpreted and led to programmes of compensatory education to 'make up for' children's 'impoverished' language (Bernstein, 1973: 25). The work of Labov, who explored the logic of non-standard languages, and an increased awareness of linguistic analysis identified that it was not a restricted code but teachers' attitudes to children's language that often led to the disadvantage. (Labov, 1960)

Research into language and thought and language and learning signify one reason why language is so important across the curriculum; language enables children to access the curriculum and the exciting world around them.

A language-rich classroom

The need for all teachers to have language awareness and to see themselves as teachers of language has long been identified in many educational reports and initiatives. In 1975 The Bullock Report 'A Language for Life' was influential in emphasising the importance of children's personal language identity and the need for primary and secondary schools to plan for language across the curriculum. (DES, 1975) Speaking and listening was established as one of the attainment targets for English in the National Curriculum but not all statutory and non-statutory documents have identified the significance of talk. The National Literacy Strategy (DfEE, 1998) specified objectives for reading and writing but not for speaking and listening. In many cases this led to a marginalisation of speaking and listening work in English and across the curriculum. In setting out four separate strands on speaking and listening in 2006 the revised Primary Framework took some steps towards raising the profile of talk. (DCSF, 2006)

The importance of language for learning across the curriculum has been emphasised more recently in The Cambridge Primary Review of 2009. The review urges that every school should have a policy for language across the curriculum asserting that *'If language unlocks thought, then thought is enhanced and challenged when language in all its aspects is pursued with purpose and rigour in every educational context.'* (Alexander, 2009:25) In Chapter 1 you read about how, as a teacher in a primary classroom, you will have an advantage over secondary colleagues in that you will probably teach the same group of children across most of the curriculum and will be able to see first-hand how learning development can be enhanced productively through cross-curricular teaching and learning. The following case study illustrates the potential to enhance children's concept development in science through setting up structures to facilitate language.

Case Study: Setting up learning contexts for children to learn through language

Sophie is a postgraduate student on her final placement. Sophie's degree was in chemistry and she has particularly enjoyed a recent science assignment in which she explored the development of children's understanding of scientific concepts. Having observed her own children's acquisition of language, Sophie is also interested in how children continue to learn through language and is a keen proponent of the use of 'buzz partners.' Sophie is working with a Year 1 class in the summer term. The children are investigating the properties of simple materials in science. Sophie has observed the 'jigsaw' technique during her previous school experience and, although she knows it is a technique perhaps more often used in Key Stage 2, she is keen to try to set up a simple jigsaw activity to facilitate the children to use language during their science investigation.

With the help of the teaching assistant Sophie has prepared five sets of similar resources that include materials in metal, paper, plastic, wood and wool. The children, who will be developing both scientific concepts and skills, will be asked to sort the materials based on a classification of simple properties. There are twenty seven children in Sophie's class and they start the lesson in five 'home' groups. The children in each group are numbered from 1 to 5. In one group there are two children who are given the number 1 and, in another group, two children who are number 2. Sophie has planned the numbering very carefully and used the 'extra' numbers to best advantage so that two lower attaining children, Callum and Miranda, each have a partner with the same number.

The children move to a table indicated by their number to form a new group. In 'jigsawing' terminology this new group is referred to as the 'expert' group. Each expert group, at times supported by Sophie, the class teacher and the teaching assistant, investigate and then sort the materials on their table. The children identify properties such as hard, soft, shiny and rough. One group also choose the category 'see through' and enjoy using the word 'transparent' that is offered to them by Sophie. After fifteen minutes the children return to their home groups to continue the investigation as they share their 'expertise'. This time the investigation of properties is enhanced by the opportunity to 'try out' and build on previous learning. Interesting and valuable discussion evolves when the children discover that the 'expert' groups have identified and allocated some different categories. The children come to recognise, for example, that a material can be both hard *and* shiny. All the children, including Callum and Miranda, have the opportunity to articulate their discoveries from the expert group, using language to consolidate and internalise their learning. The children who have encountered the word 'transparent' are also very keen to try out their new vocabulary. Sophie is pleased with the outcome of the activity and in her

$\rightarrow$

lesson evaluation she identifies that the time spent in grouping and regrouping the children has been time well spent in enabling the children to extend their investigation as a community of learners. The children have explored the properties of the materials through talk as well as with their eyes and hands.

Links to the National Curriculum

In group discussion children carry out investigations, share ideas and comment and report on what they have discovered. They learn to take turns in speaking, relate their contributions to what has gone before and extend their ideas in the light of discussion. In science children use appropriate senses to explore materials recognising their similarities and differences. They sort objects into groups based on their assessment of simple properties. They learn to make simple comparisons, review their work and explain to others what they have done.

The provision of a classroom environment rich in language opportunity and benefitting from a variety of language models is essential to support children's learning and their continued language development. Concerns have been identified, however, about children who fail to flourish in school due to significant language challenges. In January 2011, 224,210 pupils in schools in England had statements of Special Educational Needs. That is 2.8 per cent of the school population. Just over half of these pupils are in mainstream state schools. The most prevalent type of needs amongst primary pupils (24.2 per cent) was in speech, language and communication (DfE, 2011). For these children early identification of individual needs is essential to provide the specific support that may be required so that they too can benefit from the language rich environment of the classroom and the potential to use language to access the whole curriculum.

Language and identity

In any analysis of children's language it is important to remember that language forms one of the most significant dimensions of an individual's sense of identity. When you hear someone speaking on the radio you may well have found that you very quickly develop a picture in your mind of the person's gender and ethnicity and even of the person's intelligence and role in society. These assumptions can turn out to be very close to reality, or they can be very wrong, but they do illustrate the close and complex relationship between language and society. In your role as a teacher it is very important to remember that a child's language is as important to a sense of self as gender and ethnicity. Any signs of disapproval about the child's language are likely to be very damaging because they imply disapproval of the individual and also the family group and possibly the wider community. For some of the children you teach the home language may be standard English dialect. For others it may a non-standard dialect of English or a first language other than English. All language users, however, operate on a continuum of registers; we use different versions of our language range according to the context, audience and purpose of the communication. Lockwood has compared this to having a 'wardrobe of voices' and suggested a valuable language activity to help children reflect on their personal 'wardrobe'. (Lockwood in Goodwin 2011:109) It is important to remember that one dialect or language is not linguistically superior to another. Our aim is to enable children to add to their language repertoire, not to replace the home language with standard English. Your respect for language variety, and the way in which you model this attitude for children, will be crucial to ensure that linguistic difference does not become linguistic disadvantage. The ethos you create will also be essential as you endeavour to exploit the potential of learning across the curriculum through language for all children.

Learning to use language

A further important dimension of language across the curriculum is that the subjects of the school curriculum provide a rich and varied context for children to use language. Beyond their initial language acquisition children will continue to develop their speaking and listening, and later their reading and writing, making decisions about the appropriate language use for a range of different purposes, contexts and audiences. Each curriculum subject will provide rich and varied opportunities for children to practise and develop their language use. For example in physical education children will make regular use of prepositions (under, over, through, across) in a very concrete way as they describe and evaluate how they travel on the floor and on apparatus in gymnastics. Similarly, the language of thought and hypothesis required in science can support the vocabulary development needed for logical thinking, reasoning and supposition in other subjects and in life.

Activity

Consider which subjects will provide contexts for the following examples of language use. Some contexts may occur in several subjects and some subjects will provide opportunities for more than one of the language examples below.

Subjects: Art & Design, Design Technology, English, Geography, History, ICT, Mathematics, Foreign Languages, Music, Physical Education, PSHE, Religious Education, Science.

Language opportunities to:	Language opportunities for:
<ul><li>contrast and compare</li><li>create and interpret stories</li><li>describe aesthetic qualities</li><li>describe cause and effect</li><li>describe position</li><li>describe similarity and difference</li><li>express alternative possibilities</li><li>express chronology and time</li><li>express creative ideas</li><li>express or argue a point of view</li><li>identify size and order</li><li>observe and record</li><li>persuade</li><li>pose questions</li><li>think and hypothesise</li></ul>	<ul><li>association and comparison</li><li>expressing preferences</li><li>giving instructions and determining chronological order</li><li>live talks and presentations</li><li>logical thinking, reasoning and supposition</li><li>making and evaluating</li><li>planning</li><li>questioning</li></ul>

Links to the National Curriculum

Exploration of the curriculum guidance for each subject will provide ample evidence of all the above forms of language use. Pupils will be taught the patterns of language vital to understanding and expression in different subjects and the particular technical and specialist vocabulary that each subject will require.

Learning about language

Opportunities to learn about language involve children being able to reflect on their own and others' use of language. Over time this helps to make language knowledge which is largely implicit, or subconscious, to become explicit. As established in Chapter 1, explicit knowledge is that which is understood and can be articulated. Explicit knowledge about language can put children more in control of their language use. For example, a child with explicit knowledge about different types of sentences might make more conscious choices about the most appropriate sentence structures to use according to the purpose, context and audience of the given text. Cross-curricular contexts can provide opportunity for children to reflect on, as well as use, the language examples in the activity above. Additionally, learning in other subjects can enhance children's knowledge about the nature of language and how language systems work. For example when learning another language in primary school, exploration of phrasing questions in Spanish or French can facilitate children to reflect on their equivalent use of questions in English.

Research Focus

The concept of Knowledge About Language or 'KAL' for both children and teachers was firmly established through The LINC (Language in the National Curriculum) Project (1989–1992) at the time of the first National Curriculum for English. The LINC project was set up following the publication of The Kingman Report into the Teaching of the English Language in 1988. Carter, who led the LINC project, described knowledge about language for teachers as important because it can *'sharpen teachers' appreciation of children's achievement with language as well as broaden the language opportunities they provide for pupils in the classroom.'* (Carter, 1990:3) The Kingman Report did not recommend what many expected: a return to 'old fashioned grammar teaching.' Kingman identified language as a much richer field of study. *'Round the city of Caxton, the electronic suburbs are rising. To the language of books is added the language of television and radio, the elliptical demotic of the telephone, the processed codes of the computer. As the shapes of literacy multiply, so our dependence on language increases. But if language motivates change, it is itself changed. To understand the principles on which that change takes pace should be denied to no one.'* (Kingman 1988:8) The Kingman Report established four branches of language study considered to be rich

→

for exploration in the classroom. Richmond, building on the original four branches of the Kingman Report, identified five categories for learning about language: the history of languages; language variety; the use of language in society; the systematic structures of language and the acquisition of language. (Carter, 1990:38) These categories, which became the basis for the work undertaken by the LINC project, have continued to appear in different forms in statutory and non-statutory English documents since the time of the first national curriculum for English.

There is overlap between these different dimensions of language exploration which can each be enhanced through work in different subjects of the curriculum where opportunities will often occur naturally to embed a language focus in other lessons. For example: many of the periods of history explored in KS 2 provide a context to consider the history of the English language, which has evolved with the assimilation of the language of many invaders and settlers. A geography topic comparing a contrasting country may be an opportunity to explore words that have entered the English language more recently through globalisation and migration. Language variety is also a very profitable dimension for a language focus. Language variety takes many forms: between formal and informal registers; between spoken and written modes; between dialects of the same language and between different world languages. Each of these allow for interesting investigation. Whilst the systematic structure of English may be mostly a focus of discrete English lessons, as has been seen in the activity above, different curriculum subjects provide a rich context for children to apply their learning. As later case studies will show, these different branches of learning *about* language can provide a rich and engaging dimension to work across the curriculum.

Planned and incidental language work

Language exploration can be part of other subjects as a planned activity. This might be a small element, perhaps just one lesson, of a curriculum focus in another subject or a major thread running through another topic. It is also possible for valuable reflection on language to happen almost incidentally but this will be dependent on your subject knowledge and enthusiasm for language to ensure you exploit opportunities that arise. Let's look first at some examples of incidental reflection about language.

What's in a word?

In your developing subject knowledge of English you will have been consolidating your knowledge of phonemes and graphemes and analysed these within words. You will probably also have encountered morphemes. A morpheme is the smallest independent unit of meaning in language and the study of the structure of words is known as morphology. The word 'jump' has one morpheme; one independent unit of meaning. The words 'jumping' and 'jumped' each have two morphemes. The morpheme 'jump' is a 'free' morpheme; it can stand alone and convey meaning. Some units of meaning, such as 'ing' and 'ed', cannot stand on their own.

These are known as 'bound' morphemes. Some understanding of morphology will help children to both decode and comprehend words they need to read and to predict words they need to spell. Morphology is also a very rich area for incidental language exploration across the curriculum. Identification of morphemes in words children encounter in curriculum subjects will not only enhance their language development; it can help to consolidate key concepts in their learning in the other subject. The word morpheme itself has interesting links to other curriculum subjects. Knowing that a morpheme is the smallest unit of meaning that can change the overall meaning of a word should enable you to bring some understanding to the qualities of metamorphic rocks in geography and the process of metamorphosis in science.

Activity

Consider the following words and what they have in common: century, centurion, centenary, centimetre, percent, centigrade, centipede, You will have identified the morpheme 'cent' meaning one hundred and might already be thinking about possible opportunities to link this knowledge to history, mathematics and science to enhance children's understanding. For example: 'per' 'cent' literally means 'each hundred.' Knowledge of this can help children to consolidate their understanding of work on percentages and to make important links between their work in different curriculum subjects.

Now try these. How many words can you think of that have the same free morpheme as the example given? How might you exploit this knowledge to further children's understanding of key concepts across the curriculum? Mathematics is a particularly rich area for these kinds of language connections but you should also spot some links to other subjects.

Morpheme	Words that include the morpheme	What meaning does the morpheme convey?
cent	century, centurion, centenary, centimetre, percent, centigrade, centipede	
tri		
quad		
metre		
graph		
oct		
dec		

The last examples 'oct' and 'dec' are very interesting because they have direct links to the months of the year, October and December being the eighth and tenth months of the year respectively in the old Roman calendar said to have been invented by Romulus. Similarly 'sept' conveys the old seventh month and 'nov' the ninth. The Gregorian calendar we know today has twelve months and includes the renamed months of July and August named after the Roman emperors Julius Caesar and Augustus. It is really powerful to think that exploration of the Roman and Gregorian calendars in a history topic on the Romans might inform children's mathematical concepts about octagons and decimals. Incidental language reflection such as this might only be very brief but it is enriching and valuable.

Case Study: Seizing incidental language opportunities

Bethany is a newly qualified teacher in her first term. She is teaching in Year 2. Bethany is well supported by her mentor and year leader and is being encouraged to recognise when it is valuable to build on children's interest and enthusiasm and to become more flexible in her approach to planning. In mathematics the children have been exploring the properties of triangles as part of their work on 2-D shapes. During the topic introduction Bethany asked the children which other words they knew that begin with 'tri'. The children volunteered several suggestions including triplets, the musical instrument triangle and triple jump. One of the children also offers 'trip' and Bethany has to explain very simply that it doesn't work for all words because words have entered the English language from different sources. The next day Liam arrives in school with his book of dinosaurs to show Bethany a picture of a triceratops. Liam is asked to share the picture with the class at the beginning of mathematics and there is discussion about the dinosaur's three horns. This prompts Katie to tell the class that her little brother has just started to ride a tricycle. Bethany decides to capitalise on the children's enthusiasm for finding words with the morpheme 'tri' by using an art lesson to create a display of objects, people and animals linked to the theme of three. The children use a range of materials including paint, printing and collage to depict musical and mathematical triangles, triceratops, trios of different objects, triplets and tricycles.

Bethany's spontaneous art lesson shows the benefit of building on children's interests and also illustrates the potential to foster key concepts through a focus on incidental language exploration. During her own research on the morpheme 'tri' Bethany has discovered three panel art paintings known as 'triptych'. Bethany can see links to art and religious education and the possibility of a more advanced exploration of 'tri' with older pupils.

Bethany's exploration of the morpheme 'tri' and the subsequent art display arose without planning. As personal subject knowledge about language develops, opportunities to explore morphology may actually becomes less incidental as opportunities will be anticipated in advance even though they may still be presented very spontaneously to the children.

Links to the National Curriculum

In reading and spelling children explore words with common spelling patterns and use their knowledge of word families to inform their understanding. They begin to develop awareness of language roots and the origins of words.

In mathematics children use the correct vocabulary to identify shapes and to describe their properties.

In art children represent their observations and ideas using a range of materials and processes.

Incidental language exploration is powerful but we cannot assume that all learning about language will take place in this way. More deliberate planning to ensure children have varied opportunities to learn about language is also very important. Whether your school operates a 'creative' or 'spiral' curriculum, as discussed in Chapter 1, it will be necessary to have a curriculum map that plots where learning about language will occur in other subjects. Awareness of the different dimensions of language study, such as the history of languages or language variety will also need to be considered to ensure that children have a broad experience of what it means to learn about language. As identified above, planned language work might be a major thread running through another topic or perhaps just one lesson linked to another subject. The following case study illustrates how children can learn about language through using material from another subject, in this example religious education, to engage in a brief exploration of language change.

Case Study: Planning a brief language activity to accompany other curriculum work

Aoife is a Year 2 undergraduate student who has enjoyed drawing children's attention to features of language as they arise incidentally across the curriculum and is keen to develop her own growing interest of language through a planned activity. She is on her second school experience working with a mixed ability Year 6 class. After discussion with the class teacher and the RE co-ordinator Aoife plans a one lesson language activity to explore three different versions of The Parable of The Good Samaritan. She uses the internet to find a version of the parable as translated by Wycliffe in 1382 and the version from the King James Bible of 1611. She already has the New International Version of the parable (1979) and the illustrated children's version which the children have been exploring in religious education through drama and discussion. The children have been reflecting on the lives of people with different values and customs and sharing their thoughts on how they can offer help to others in need. They have also thought about how different groups sometimes find it very difficult to help each. When they were in Year 5 the children had completed a scheme of work exploring where the Bible

$\rightarrow$

comes from so the RE co-ordinator has explained to Aoife that this will be a good opportunity to revisit some of the children's learning from this earlier work but this time with a particular language focus.

Aoife begins the lesson by asking the children to share what they remember about the historic journey and development of the Bible. She then introduces the lesson objective, which is to explore how the English language has changed through different versions of the parable, and distributes three versions of the parable to each of the six groups. The children are asked to try to place the different versions in the order they were written. The teaching assistant works with the less able group. The children volunteer their suggestions for the historical chronology of the three texts sharing some of the features they have noticed to justify the order in which they have placed the three versions. Having clarified the correct order and given some brief information about the Wycliffe and King James Bibles, Aoife uses the interactive whiteboard to model some of the features she would like the children to look at more closely in the role of 'language detectives'. They are asked to focus on vocabulary, spelling and sentence structure.

Aoife's focus questions are: 1. Can you find any words from the older versions that are no longer in common usage? 2. Which words are still in use but now have a different spelling? And 3: Are there any changes in the way the sentences are structured? Aoife uses the three examples of Line 35 to model the detective work, identifying the language features on which she has chosen to focus.

1. *Haue the cure of hym; and what euer thou schalt yyue ouer, Y schal yelde to thee, whanne Y come ayen.'* (Wycliffe)

2. *'Take care of him; and whatsoever thou spendest more, when I come again, I will repay thee. '* (King James)

3. *'Look after him,'* he said, *'and when I return, I will reimburse you for any extra expense you may have.'* (New International Version)

Aoife identifies the change from 'hym' to 'him' and 'yelde' (yield) to 'repay' and then to 'reimburse'. The children also notice the change in the order of the clauses with 'when I come again' and 'when I return' appearing earlier in the sentence in the King James and New International versions. There is discussion about the word 'yield' with children contributing examples of when they have heard the word used. Aoife also models exploration of the expression *'Haue the cure of hym'*, replaced in the later versions by *'Take care of him'* and *'Look after him.'*

The children are very keen to begin their detective task and work in small groups to catalogue the changes they can identify. There is lively discussion about spelling changes which leads one group to also talk about the spelling they use in text

→

messages and whether or not correct spelling matters if spelling changes over time. After twenty minutes each group feeds back to the rest of the class sharing some of the language and spelling changes that they have found. Aoife uses the interactive whiteboard to display a version from *The Message*, which uses quite colloquial language. *'Take good care of him. If it costs any more, put it on my bill—I'll pay you on my way back.'* (*The Message*: 1993) This leads to interesting discussion about why there have been, and continue to be, so many versions of the Bible. The children make thoughtful observations about the relevance of the Bible to millions of people across the world today and in the past. They share further recollections of their work on the journey of the Bible from the previous year.

To conclude, Aoife poses some questions about where else the children may have seen older versions of English. The children share knowledge about churches and graveyards and visits they have made to museums and castles and Brian offers to ask his mum if he can bring an old family Bible to school for others to see.

Aoife's objective for the lesson was for the children to understand the broad principle that words, their meanings and spellings, have changed over time rather than for them to remember the precise detail of the changes but the children have enjoyed identifying the specific examples they found in their detective role. The language exploration focus has drawn on the dimensions of the history of languages and, particularly in looking at the colloquial version of *The Message*, the dimension of language variety.

Aoife's lesson was a brief language activity to accompany other curriculum work but there would be ample scope to develop the ideas further in both RE and English and also through history and art. There might be opportunity to explore further examples of older English in the local community through a visit to a churchyard or an historic site. The children could explore historical manuscripts and take a closer look at the historical contexts of the different versions of the Bible. Children enjoy creating illuminated letters and might do this for their own version of The Good Samaritan or for other creative work such as poetry. A particularly challenging task might be for some children to try to retell The Good Samaritan story in text writing or to explore online versions of the parable in other languages. For bilingual children in the class, versions in other languages could also provide an interesting context to share something of their personal language repertoire.

Links to the National Curriculum

In group discussion children explore, clarify and extend ideas. They are able to deal with tentative suggestions, review what has been said and summarise the main points of a discussion. They understand the relevance of the roots and origins of words and are able to identify grammatical structures in sentences. They understand that words and expressions change over time and are able to make use of a simple etymological dictionary.

In religious education children think about what sacred texts and other sources say about God, the world and human life. They explore the lives of people living in other places and times, and people with different values and customs. They reflect on ideas of right and wrong and their own and others' responses to them. They reflect on social, cultural, religious and ethnic diversity in Britain and the wider world and the important contribution religion can make to community cohesion and the combating of religious prejudice and discrimination.

Planning for language study to be a significant thread running through another subject

A language focus can be a major thread running through a topic in another subject. History is an excellent example of this because the English language has evolved in part due to the influence of different invaders and settlers, many of which form part of the history curriculum in primary school. This brief summary of the history of the English language should enable you to identify some of the many opportunities that could arise to link history and English.

History of the English language

Most of the European languages spoken today, including English, belong to the Indo-European family of languages which evolved across Europe and southern Asia before 3,000 BC. Although there are no written records of Indo-European, linguists are able to trace common roots through words such as mētēr (Greek), mater (Latin), mutter (German), moeder (Dutch) and similarly pater (Latin), vater (German) and pitr (Sanskrit). These are all 'cognates,' or similar words, for the English words mother and father.

Latin and what are known as the Romance languages, including French, form one branch of the Indo-European family. People often assume incorrectly that English originates from Latin but English is actually from the Germanic branch of the Indo-European family which includes modern day German, Dutch and Flemish. Latin has influenced the English we use today through the Roman occupation of Britain and later the Norman Conquest, after which time French became the official language of England for two hundred years.

The early inhabitants of England were Celtic speaking. During the fifth and sixth centuries England was invaded by tribes from Germany and Denmark including the Angles (from whom we get the name England), the Saxons and later the Vikings. The Celts were pushed out to Cornwall, Wales, Scotland and Ireland influencing the Welsh and Gaelic languages we know today.

The English spoken after the time of these invasions is known as 'Old English' which existed in dialect versions in different parts of the country. The best known example of Old English is the epic poem Beowulf. The Old English dialect of King Alfred eventually evolved into the Middle English of the twelfth century. Latin retained some influence through the church and early versions of the Bible. When William the Conqueror invaded England in 1066 he brought with him an old French language of Latin roots but also further Germanic language influences through the heritage of the 'Norsemen' or Normans. After the time of the Norman Conquest the noblemen would speak French and the commoners English. Over time a combination of these two languages developed into what linguists term 'Middle English.' The works of Chaucer are written in Middle English, which eventually became the official language of parliament and the court. We would recognise many of the sounds, spellings, word endings and word order of Middle English. Middle English evolved into 'Modern English' from the 1500s onwards. Many classical Latin and Greek words were absorbed into the language during the Renaissance. It may surprise you to know that the works of Shakespeare are in Modern English! The first ever book to be printed in English was published by William Caxton in 1473, the printing revolution eventually opening a world of literacy to the masses. This led ultimately to the standardisation of English, based on the dialect of London, and the publication of the first English dictionary, *'Cawdrey's Table Alphabetical'*, in 1604. Dr Samuel Johnson's famous *'Dictionary of the English Language'* was published in 1755.

If you are planning work on Britain from the 1930s it would be valuable to explore the influence of American English with the placement of many American GIs in the United Kingdom during the Second World War and also the influence of the Hollywood film industry. Local history study can also be a vehicle for learning about language and can support exploration of the local area.

Is it wrong to borrow and not give back?

Aoife's language work in the last Case Study explored the dimension of language change over time and concluded by raising children's awareness to the continual nature of this change. One way in which English continues to evolve is through the absorption of words from other languages. Similarly many English words are adopted into other languages. This phenomena of semantic change is often referred to as 'borrowing' but, as Crystal explains, this is not a very appropriate term as the words are never given back! (Crystal 2002: 332) Exploration of 'borrowed' words has strong links to globalisation, migration and learning about distant places in geography and also to PSHE because it can help to raise the status of the home or heritage languages of children in the class. It is also an important area of language awareness for children in monolingual schools because the wider society in which all children in the United Kingdom live is becoming increasingly multilingual. The route of borrowed words into English can be complicated because words have often been borrowed and absorbed through several languages before reaching English. Many words have entered English from French having been previously absorbed into French from Italian or directly from Latin. Many Latin words had Ancient Greek routes. The word 'pilot' for example, for someone who steers a ship, was borrowed into English in the sixteenth century from the French word *'pilote'*. The French 'pilote' had derived from the medieval Latin 'pilotus', an evolution of 'pēdot' from the Greek pēdon. The word *'pepper'* is another complicated example. 'Pepper' is from the Old English *'piper'* or *'pipor'*, of West Germanic origin. This is related to the Dutch *'peper'* and German *'Pfeffer'* which migrated via Latin from the Greek *'peperi'* and the Sanskrit *'pippalī'*. A good etymological dictionary, which explores the origins of words, will be an essential classroom resource. Etymology can also be researched online. The Oxford Dictionary (OED online) is an excellent source. (www.oxforddictionaries.com)

Activity

The words below have been absorbed into English from six different languages: Arabic, Dutch, French, Greek, Hindi and Italian. There are six words from each language. Try to predict the language from which each word has been 'borrowed.' Some words will probably be easy to predict but some may surprise you.

Match six 'borrowed' words to each language: Arabic, Dutch, French, Greek, Hindi, Italian. One word from each language has been identified to get you started.

ballerina	confetti	jodhpurs	spaghetti
beige *(French)*	cot *(Hindi)*	jumper	sugar *(Arabic)*
Bible	deer *(Dutch)*	machine	tarantula *(Italian)*
biscuit	easel	magazine	tennis
boss	elephant	opera	thesaurus *(Greek)*
bungalow	garage	rhombus	tulip
butler	giraffe	scarlet	umbrella
cheetah	golf	shampoo	veranda
coffee	horizon	skipper	wagon

The answers are given at the end of the chapter on page 38. You can use an etymological dictionary or the OED online to discover the historic journey of each of the words into English.

As children begin to learn about the history of Great Britain and the nature of language change, they may not be surprised to discover that words have been absorbed into English from Greek, Latin, Italian and French but may be surprised that words have been borrowed from Arabic or that the familiar word 'pyjamas' is from Hindi and Urdu. Activities which explore the language origin of words offer a valuable opportunity to raise the profile of non-European languages, some of which may be spoken by members of the class or wider community.

There are many resources to support language across the curriculum and some suggestions for further reading are given at the end of this chapter. Remember, one of the richest resources is the children themselves. The children you teach will be a living embodiment of different varieties of English and possibly other languages. We have explored how language changes and this is not something which just happened in the past: it is happening now. Children and teenagers are significant agents for language change and each generation has its 'buzz' words and expressions. You might not have used vocabulary such as *'spiffing'*, *'top-hole'*, *'groovy'* or *'fab'* but you might have used *'wicked'* in a different way from your parents. Listen to the children you teach and discover how they are using language differently from you.

Learning Outcomes Review

This chapter has explored the importance of language across the curriculum and considered how children learn through language, how they learn to use language and how they learn about language. Key principles have been established for planned and incidental language work and specific cross-curricular opportunities for language activities have been identified. The case studies have cited several examples from practice and shown how these relate to the curriculum.

Self-assessment questions

1. How will you ensure that children have opportunities to learn through language and to use language in their learning?
2. How have the activities and case studies in this chapter developed your awareness of what is meant by learning about language?
3. How can you begin to plan for language exploration across the curriculum?
4. Are there curriculum subjects not explored in this chapter where you have already identified the potential for planned or incidental language work?

Answers to activity on page 37.

Activity answers: words 'borrowed' from other languages and absorbed into English. Match six 'borrowed' words to each language: Arabic, Dutch, French, Greek, Hindi, Italian.			
ballerina (*Italian*)	confetti (*Italian*)	jodhpurs (*Hindi*)	spaghetti (*Italian*)
beige (*French*)	cot (*Hindi*)	jumper (*Arabic*)	sugar (*Arabic*)
Bible (*Greek*)	deer (*Dutch*)	machine (*Greek*)	tarantula (*Italian*)
biscuit (*French*)	easel (*Dutch*)	magazine (*Arabic*)	tennis (*French*)
boss (*Dutch*)	elephant (*Greek*)	opera (*Italian*)	thesaurus (*Greek*)
bungalow (*Hindi*)	garage (*French*)	rhombus (*Greek*)	tulip (*French*)

butler *(French)*	giraffe *(Arabic)*	scarlet *(Arabic)*	umbrella *(Italian)*
cheetah *(Hindi)*	golf *(Dutch)*	shampoo *(Hindi)*	veranda *(Hindi)*
coffee *(Arabic)*	horizon *(Greek)*	skipper *(Dutch)*	wagon *(Dutch)*

Some of the answers above may surprise you. You may have predicted for example that 'tulip' has been imported from the Dutch language. Tulip, however, evolved from the French *tuilipe*, via Turkish from the Persion *dulband* 'tuban' which depicts the shape of the flower.

Further Reading

These titles are a useful starting point to develop your subject knowledge and to inform exploration of language across the curriculum.

British Library Sound Archive http://sounds.bl.uk/Accents-and-dialects and http://www.bl.uk/learning/langlit/sounds/index.html

Bryson, B. (1990) *Mother Tongue: The English Language*. London: Penguin Books.

Crystal, D. (2007) *How Language Works*. London: Penguin Books.

Dalby, A. (2006) *Dictionary of languages: the definitive reference to more than 400 languages*. London: A & C Black Publishers Ltd.

Gulland, D.M. and Hinds-Howell, D. (1994) *The Penguin Dictionary of English Idioms*. London: Penguin Books.

Kacirk, J. (1999) *Forgotten English*. USA, Quill: William Morrow.

Mills, A.D. (2011) *A Dictionary of British Place Names*. Oxford: Oxford University Press.

Room, A. (2000) *Cassell's Foreign Words and Phrases*. London: Cassell.

References

Alexander, R. et al. (2009) *Children, their World, their Education. Final Report and Recommendations of the Cambridge Primary Review*. Oxford: Routledge.

Bernstein, B. (1973) *Class, codes and control, Volume 2. Applied studies towards a sociology of language*. Routledge and Kegan Paul.

Bruner, J.S. (2006) *In search of pedagogy/Jerome S. Bruner. Vol. 2, The selected works of Jerome S. Bruner*. London: Routledge.

Bullock, A. (1975) *The Bullock Report. A language for life*. London: HMSO. Available at: www.educationengland.org.uk/documents/bullock

Carter, R.A. (ed) (1990) *Knowledge About Language and The Curriculum: The LINC Reader*. London: Hodder & Stoughton.

Crystal, D. (2002) *The Cambridge Encyclopedia of Language*. Cambridge: Cambridge University Press.

DCSF (2006) *The Primary National Strategies*. The Stationery Office.

De Bono, Edward (1970) *Lateral thinking: A Textbook of Creativity*. London: Ward Lock.

DES (1989) *Cox Report: the Report of the National Curriculum English Working Group*. London: DES.

DES (1989) *English for ages 5 to 16: Proposals of the Secretary of State for Education and Science and the Secretary of State for Wales*. UK: HMSO.

DES (1990) *English in the National Curriculum (no. 2)*. UK: HMSO.

DfE (2011) Statistical First Release www.education.gov.uk/rsgateway/DB/SFR/s001007/sfr14-2011v2.pdf

DfEE (1998) *The National Literacy Strategy: Framework for Teaching*. The Stationery Office.

DfEE (1999) *The National Curriculum handbook for primary teachers in England in key stages 1 and 2*. London: The Stationery Office.

Halliday, M.A.K. (1975) *Learning How to Mean – Explorations in the Development of Language*. London: Edward Arnold.

Kingman, J. (1988) *The Kingman Report. Report of the Committee of Inquiry into the Teaching of English Language*. London: HMSO. Available at:www.educationengland.org.uk/documents/kingman/kingman00.html

Labov, W. (1972) *Sociolinguistic Patterns*. Oxford: Basil Blackwell.

Labov, W. (1969) *The logic of non-standard English*. In Mercer, N. *Language and Literacy from an Educational Perspective*. Milton Keynes: Open University Press.

Lockwood, M. (2011) *Opening the Wardrobe of Voices: standard English and language variation at key stage 2*. In Goodwin, P. *The Literate Classroom* (3rd edn). London: David Fulton.

NavPress Publishing Group http://www.navpress.com/

Piaget, J. (1926; 1959) *The Language and Thought of the Child*. London: Routledge & Kegan Paul.

The Holy Bible (1979) *New International Version; Containing the Old Testament and the New Testament*. London: Hodder & Stoughton.

The Oxford Dictionary Online www.oxforddictionaries.com

Vygotsky, L.S. (1978) *Mind and Society: The Development of Higher Mental Processes*. Cambridge, MA: Harvard University Press.

Wells, G. (1986) *The Meaning Makers: Children Learning Language and Using Language to Learn*. London: Heinemann.

3. Literature across the curriculum

Learning Outcomes

This chapter aims to help you to:

- consider the importance of providing a broad and diverse range of literature in your classroom;
- become aware of the cross-curricular potential of children's literature;
- begin to understand how texts can be used to support cross-curricular learning;
- be introduced to some examples of using literature across the curriculum;
- consider how and why you might use literature to support cross-curricular learning in your own classroom.

TEACHERS' STANDARDS

A teacher must:

1. **Set high expectations which inspire, motivate and challenge pupils**
- establish a safe and stimulating environment for pupils, rooted in mutual respect
- set goals that stretch and challenge pupils of all backgrounds, abilities and dispositions

2. **Promote good progress and outcomes by pupils**
- demonstrate knowledge and understanding of how pupils learn and how this impacts on teaching

3. **Demonstrate good subject and curriculum knowledge**
- have a secure knowledge of the relevant subject(s) and curriculum areas, foster and maintain pupils' interest in the subject and address misunderstandings
- demonstrate an understanding of and take responsibility for promoting high standards of literacy

4. **Plan and teach well structured lessons**
- contribute to the design and provision of an engaging curriculum within the relevant subject area(s)

5. **Adapt teaching to respond to the strengths and needs of all pupils**
- know when and how to differentiate appropriately, using approaches which enable pupils to be taught effectively
- have a clear understanding of the needs of all pupils, including those with special educational needs; those of high ability; those with English as an additional language; those with disabilities; and be able to use and evaluate distinctive teaching approaches to engage and support them

Introduction

It is imperative that children are introduced to a broad, diverse selection of literature and that their experience of texts encompasses a range of genres. This enables children a rich and positive experience of literature and has the potential to inspire, excite and enthuse children. This chapter explores how you can teach and stimulate children through literature, making relevant and advantageous cross-curricular links.

Choice of texts

It should be noted that the texts suggested in this chapter are a starting point only. The recommendations are to guide and offer suggestions while you begin considering the interests, preferences and needs of the children you teach. The texts outlined in the case studies are selected not only for their potential to enhance learning across the curriculum, but also because they are examples of excellent, high quality and enjoyable literature to share with children. It is important that in your attempts to make cross-curricular links you do not neglect the prerequisite to use inspiring, quality texts. As you become increasingly familiar with children's literature, you will develop expertise in this area and be able to recommend and select high quality, engaging and enjoyable texts for yourself and for the children you teach.

Why focus on children's literature?

Children can be extremely motivated by literature and its excavation and exploration is academically, socially and emotionally enriching. Exploring literature and its layers of meaning enhances understanding and develops a range of analytical and literacy skills. Furthermore, such exploration has the power to transform and to enable children to think about situations and concepts they might otherwise not.

Using literature to introduce or explore cross-curricular concepts

In the case study below, we meet trainee teacher Hannah who is concerned that her mathematics teaching in a Year 4 class relies on worksheets to develop children's mathematical skills. She is keen to find a more creative way of reinforcing and practising these skills. She explores two picture books with the children and finds that these stimulate interest and discussion as well as providing excellent opportunities for follow-up work and engaging mathematics activities.

> ### Case Study: Using literature to initiate mathematical investigations
>
> *One Grain of Rice* by Demi is a mathematically-rich folk tale, set long ago in India. Firstly, Hannah explores the illustrations in the book, asking the children to consider similarities in artistic techniques and distinctive features they may have
>
> $\rightarrow$

seen before. They have been looking at art from around the world, so this immediately involves the children who recognise the traditional painting style within the book. They also consider the use of symbolism and the appearance of different animals in the illustrations.

The Raja in the story was respected, but kept nearly all of the people's rice for himself, even when famine struck. Hannah introduced the geographical aspects of learning to ensure that the children understood famine and why it might occur. They also discussed famines that have occurred both historically and more recently, developing global awareness but not portraying famine as something that only happens in other parts of the world.

A village girl called Rani devises a clever plan which culminates in the Rajah agreeing to give her one grain of rice which is doubled every day for thirty days. The children are set the mathematical task of predicting and estimating the final total. They are then read the story and work out day by day how much the rice increases. This activity develops their skills in doubling and cumulative mathematics.

Further challenges are set as extension opportunities and group tasks requiring children to work out the totals if the rice was multiplied by four each day, or started as three grains of rice and so on. Some children publish picture books with similar mathematical stories they have created.

365 Penguins by Jean-Luc Fromental and Joelle Jolivet is Hannah's second book choice. In this story, a penguin is delivered to a family one day and to their surprise another is delivered every day after that for a year. One challenge for the children is to estimate and then work out how many penguins occupy the household as weeks and eventually months go by. The picture book also presents problems such as dividing the penguins to store them in groups of twelve and so on.

An environmental theme is included, as it materialises that the deliveries are the work of an ecologist uncle who is attempting to reverse the fate of the creatures being adversely affected by global warming. Hannah asks the children to research penguins and their natural habitats, locations and needs. This is discussed in relation to the problems facing the family required to house the penguins. Work on global warming and advocacy ensues and the children develop their knowledge and understanding of environmental issues and geographical factors. This leads to independent research projects on other environmental issues and wildlife concerns.

Creative writing develops as Hannah asks the children to write from different perspectives: the penguins', different members of the family and the uncle's. She

$\longrightarrow$

first involves the children in role play and hot-seating to explore these different perspectives.

The children write letters to environmental lobbying groups and members of parliament sharing what they have learned about the plight of the penguins and advocating positive action to prevent such ecological disaster.

This case study presents examples of the opportunities for cross-curricular learning focusing on the exploration of mathematics and geographical concepts through literature. Important issues such as global warming and environmental damage are addressed in an accessible and non-threatening manner which both engages and edifies the children. The potential of this is discussed further in Chapter 10.

Links to the National Curriculum

As well as speaking and listening as the children explored different viewpoints through drama research was conducted which enabled the children to read for information. The children's writing was also developed.

The art focus through the exploration of *One Grain of Rice* ensured that the children were evaluating and developing work. Children also developed knowledge and understanding of art elements, materials and processes and the roles of illustrators.

Geography NC links were made through exploring the contexts of the books and their settings as well as habitats and ecology. The children developed their geographical enquiry and skills by asking questions, collecting and analysing evidence and using appropriate vocabulary. Knowledge and understanding of places was developed and their knowledge and understanding of patterns and processes was enhanced and they could explain these. Environmental change and sustainable development were studied in depth and the children understood how people can improve and damage environments and the effects of this. They also explored the importance of managing environments sustainably and became involved in campaigning for this.

Links to NC mathematics are numerous. The children engaged in problem solving and explained their reasoning. Their understanding of numbers and the number system was enhanced, including number sequences. They were able to use number patterns to make predictions. Calculation skills were developed and written methods were employed. The children were involved in solving and checking their answers to numerical problems.

Using literature to explore emotions and experiences

Children's literature provides a safe forum in which to explore serious or sensitive issues or problems, both familiar and unfamiliar. Thus, exploring literature can deepen understanding, make sense of experiences, open new worlds and viewpoints to children, allow them to consider different perspectives and possibilities and generally enliven their imaginations. Empathy can be developed through exploring the different circumstances, attitudes and beliefs presented in literature. Literature has the power to transport children to other situations and to enable them to delve further into their own. As one seminal expert on children's reading, Margaret Meek, summarises, good readers *find in books the depth and breadth of human experience* (1982, p17).

In the case study below, Sophie is working on an art topic studying contemporary artists with a Year 5 class during her final school placement. She investigates the work of Jean-Michel Basquiat through the book *Life Doesn't Frighten Me* which features the artist's paintings and the words of Maya Angelou.

Case Study: Focusing on art

On first reading the book to the class, Sophie does not show them the illustrations, focusing instead on the words which are poetic and have a rhyming pattern. The children explore the rhythm of the poem and its structure. Sophie encourages them to clap in time to the pattern of the words and to explore the syllables as well as the repetition. The children focus on the literary techniques and their effects while they explore the poetry. The effectiveness of this genre is discussed and suggestions are offered as to why the author chose this particular approach.

A subsequent music lesson allows the children, in groups, to compose and perform musical accompaniment for the poem, creating a song using the text of *Life Doesn't Frighten Me* as the lyrics. The majority of the class decide that the language is best suited to a rap and compose and perform accordingly.

This is then developed by the children in small groups to create a dance. They perform this to each other and evaluate their own and others' performances.

Sophie encourages sensitive discussion and sharing of issues raised within the book. The poem depicts a lack of fear but describes situations and things that are in fact very frightening. The children's PSHE work centres on fears and the hiding or rejecting of these and reasons behind both the fears and their denial. The children share things that have frightened them and strategies for coping with fear. Sophie uses circle time to ensure that all children's contributions are heard and awarded equal value.

Having explored the literary devices and their effects and discussed thoroughly the vocabulary used and choice of language, Sophie asks the children to predict and

→

discuss the possible illustrations that might accompany the text. An art task enables the class to illustrate the book with their own ideas, sketching and painting their own creations to accompany the text which Sophie has provided for each child with blank spaces to add illustrations. The children's books are celebrated by being displayed in the school entrance hall.

The next week, Sophie reads the book to the class whilst simultaneously displaying the text and illustrations on the IWB. Prior to this, she asks the children which artist might have illustrated this book and why. Discussion around styles of art work and popular contemporary artists is rich. The children are very excited and often surprised by the art work in the book. Although they were familiar with the work of Basquiat, Sophie had not shared with them that the book featured his art. They discuss the distinctive nature of his work and the textures, colours and images that are identified within it. Careful observation and analysis of the illustrations forms the focus of the rest of the class work related to *Life Doesn't Frighten Me*.

Sophie is now planning a range of English work around the book.

It is clear from this case study that there is immeasurable potential to explore emotion and experience through children's literature. The discussion elicited by this book provides opportunity for children to engage with concepts and feelings with sensitivity and maturity. Mutual respect is developed as children open up about personal experiences and feelings. The honest exploration of children's own emotions is enhanced by the context of experiencing an author's and artist's own sharing of feelings. Literature can provide the window to other people's thoughts which enables children to explore their own.

Links to the National Curriculum

There are direct links to PSHE as the children talked about themselves and issues and considered other points of view.

Music was incorporated as the children learned to control sounds through singing and playing and developed their performance skills. They also developed composing skills in creating and developing their musical ideas and making choices. The children explored and explained their own ideas and feelings about the music and used dance to develop this.

The children created and performed controlled dances using a range of movements to a high quality. They developed knowledge, skills and understanding in evaluating and improving performance within Physical Education.

In relation to art and design, the children explored and developed ideas and investigated and created art work themselves. They were able to evaluate Basquiat's work and talk about how they thought and felt about it. Knowledge and understanding about elements, processes and artists was developed through the sequence of work that Sophie had planned and taught.

The right texts for the children you teach

First and foremost it is important to state that the power and potential of literature is dependent both on the quality of texts and the selection of the 'right' texts for children. This is not to suggest that there are recommended books that are appropriate and advisable for all children to read; in fact the contrary is true. Your role as a trainee teacher is to find the literature that will appeal to and stimulate the children you are teaching. It is incumbent upon you to discover the children's interests, delve into their personal preferences and source and provide the literature that will excite, enthuse and motivate them. Reading is very personal and preferences will vary; you must treat each child as an individual and aim to find and provide the 'right' texts for each child. As you get to know your class and the individuals within it, this will become easier and you can experiment with texts, presenting the full range of genres and widening the children's experience by providing a varied and abundant literary diet.

Some points to consider when using children's literature for cross-curricular learning

Although this chapter focuses on using literature as a vehicle for cross-curricular learning, it is vital that literature is not used solely as a teaching tool or viewed only as a device to develop children's skills. Although there is value in exploiting, in a positive sense, the potential of children's literature, this should not be the sole purpose for its inclusion in your teaching. It is essential that literature is regularly enjoyed solely for its own sake and that an attitude of finding joy and gratification in reading is modelled and encouraged. Try to keep in mind that literature, from all genres, should be provided for children's pleasure as well as for their learning. Children must be encouraged to explore literature for no other reason but to gain delight and entertainment from it.

It is crucial to encourage reading and the exploration of literature beyond the classroom. Research suggests that this can be achieved, in part, through a positive, celebratory and enabling approach to using and sharing literature (Fox, 1992; Goodwin, 2008; Chambers, 1995). Celebrating literature through the environment and ethos you create is fundamental to effective exploration of and cross-curricular learning through literature. Displays, the availability of resources including literature and a positive attitude are all significant factors. However, the potential of literature to enable access to learning across the curriculum is extensive and can be successfully utilised while simultaneously motivating children to explore and enjoy.

Children should be encouraged not only to read a range of texts, but also to develop and articulate their own tastes and preferences in reading. They must be supported to try unfamiliar texts and be guided towards sampling a range of genres, but not forced to persevere with texts they are not enjoying or interested in. A positive attitude to reading is encouraged through modelling an affirmative, relaxed and open-minded approach to sharing texts and opinions about these texts. It is important to encourage children's experiences of literature, without any mandatory or punitive aspects to your expectations. In this way, children are likely to develop a more positive attitude towards and increased confidence in their reading as well as becoming more discerning in their choices of literature.

Research Focus

Much has been written about the importance of being literate and within this, the value of reading. Although there is much recent research to keep up to date with, it is first necessary to revisit the influential work of those in the field who have contributed greatly to our current understanding of how children become readers and writers.

One seminal author in this field is Margaret Meek, who, writing the 1980s and 1990s, established the connection between literature and literacy. Her influences include Frank Smith, who claimed that children learn to read by reading (1985), an assumption that Meek perpetuates (1982, p11).

In her text *How Texts Teach What Readers Learn* (1988), Meek advocates letting the text teach the reader (1998, p38) which reminds us of the importance of exploration and enjoyment of books. She also asserts... *the reading of stories makes skilful, powerful readers who come to understand not only the meaning but also the force of texts* (1988, p40). This is worth remembering in the context of cross-curricular learning.

Meek makes the link between reading and writing as it is through reading that writers emerge and develop. Donald Graves is a seminal author in the area of children's writing and his work from the 1980s should be explored to understand how this has influenced more recent research and current thinking.

The importance of literature in developing writing is considered, among many other places, in Pam Czerniewska's book *Learning About Writing* (1992). She recognises and reminds us of the value of the wealth of experience children bring to the classroom, as was touched upon in Chapter 1.

In the following case study, Sally's Year 2 class have been enjoying fairy stories and traditional tales and are quite familiar with many popular classics. Sally chooses to share *Jeremiah in the Dark Woods* by Janet and Allan Ahlberg in order to develop the children's understanding of narrative structure and literary techniques. Her focus is on English as her school's policy is to teach through single subject coverage. She is able to incorporate drama to enhance learning.

Case Study: Developing reading and writing

Jeremiah in the Dark Woods is a story with a familiar pattern, hence Sally's decision to explore narrative structure through it. The children will eventually use the structure of this story to create their own stories in this genre.

Jeremiah in the Dark Woods features many familiar characters and elements of traditional tales, so Sally spends a lot of time discussing who appears and why they are already familiar. The children predict how each character will unfold in the story and extensive character analysis and exploration arises as the children draw on their knowledge of other stories and the roles and personalities of each character within these. Simple analysis of literary devices and structures is encouraged and the children are able to consider the authors' style as well as their intent.

Sally also spends a lot of time on role play, hot-seating and conscience alley activities to develop the children's learning and deepen their understanding of the characters through drama.

The learning culminates in some beautifully written and illustrated stories which Sally makes into a book to be kept in the book corner and shared by all.

In the case study above, children's writing is developed through the focus on reading and discussing the text. The children are made aware of literary devices, authorial techniques and narrative structure and style and thus are more able to experiment with and gain control of these in their own writing.

Links to the National Curriculum

Sally's focus is English. For example, she involves the children in developing their speaking and listening including group discussion and interaction and drama activities enhance their learning. The children use and enhance their knowledge of book conventions, structure and sequence, drawing on their own understanding of the content of the story. They were also enhancing their understanding of literature and responding imaginatively to this. The learning culminated in the creation and publication of stories written by each child.

The importance of talking about literature

Children can effectively access the cross-curricular themes of the texts presented in this chapter alongside thorough and positive exploration of the texts themselves. Focusing on the literature and allowing children to respond to it is the most important premise. Discussion of the themes, the language, the illustrations and the text is crucial. It is important that children's responses are encouraged and respected and that they are provided the forum and enabled the skills and language to coherently and honestly discuss, appraise and respond to what they read or hear read to them.

Research suggests that opportunities for talk are fundamental to enhancing writing (Corbett, 2008; Chambers, 1986; Dawes and Birrell, 2000; Palmer, 2011). It can be argued that discussion is pivotal to effective learning in general. Encouraging children to share literature with each other, recommend books and discuss preferences is paramount in the journey towards articulate book talk and effective learning through literature. Respecting different opinions and responses is essential and as a teacher you must encourage and model this consistently.

Using a range of literature

As previously mentioned, a range of literature and genres should be enthusiastically promoted and readily available. The texts explored in this chapter present some variety, but it should be recognised that the full range cannot be presented here. Non-fiction texts are not considered in this chapter as these will be explored further in Chapter 4. You will need to become familiar with genres of fiction and the diversity of texts, so the Further Reading focus at the end of this chapter provides some starting points to help you to explore this. You should aim to present and celebrate a range of genres including poetry, myths and legends, traditional tales and contemporary stories. Picture books can be explored at any age and these can be examined at different levels, with distinct foci, to ensure age appropriateness. You might want to consider also whether you will include comics and digital media in the range of possibilities. Children can explore film and perhaps comparing and contrasting the book and film version of a novel can stimulate some very interesting learning. There is no reason why visual literature cannot be used. In fact it is imperative that the different needs, preferences and learning styles of children are considered and provided for and it is positive to be open to and not limit children's experiences of the whole range of possibilities available.

Research Focus

Debate around children's reading is frequently very topical and is no less pertinent at the present time. In response to this debate, some interesting research has recently been undertaken which is particularly relevant to this chapter's assertion that a range of literature should be presented to and enjoyed with children.

Cremin et al. focused on teachers and their own knowledge of texts and thus their ability to use a range of literature in the classroom. *The study explored teachers' reading habits and preferences, investigated their knowledge of children's literature, and documented their reported use of such texts and involvement with library services* (2008, p449). It is of concern that the findings indicated that primary practitioners have limited knowledge of and use a very limited range of literature. The implications of this lack of repertoire are examined in the journal article 'Exploring Teachers' Knowledge of Children's Literature' (2008).

Activity

To ensure that you are familiar with a range of genres, visit your local children's library or children's section of the library and browse the selection of books available. Speak to the librarian and elicit his/her knowledge about children's books and different genres. Ask about the range of accessible books and how this is selected. What factors influence the books available? How does the librarian ensure availability of a range of books? What constitutes a range? Are there any specific titles or authors that are particularly popular? Is one genre more popular with certain age groups? Is one genre more popular at present/are there trends in popularity of different genres and what affect these? It is also worth finding out the services and resources available for schools from the children's library and librarian.

Whilst in school, ask the children about the books they read. Try to find out their favourite books or authors and what influences these choices (television series, films, peer recommendation, availability, teacher reading aloud and so on). Consider the range of books available to the children within school. How accessible are these books? Are children encouraged to explore different genres? Are there opportunities for book talk? It may be interesting to compare reading choices across different age ranges as well as in different schools or settings. Consider also your own childhood memories of favourite books and personal reading experiences and interests and any significant influences.

Diversity and inclusion

It is critical that the literature in your classroom positively represents the multicultural society in which we live and is sensitive towards and celebratory of the wider world. Children's literature is an excellent source of positive portrayals of the diversity of people and society and can present a myriad of opportunities and life choices in an accessible and normalising way. The enhanced understanding that children can gain through literature presents a perfect opportunity to develop global awareness and citizenship and this will be explored further in Chapter 9.

In the case study below, a Year 4/5 class is studying the Tudor period. Aamir, the trainee teacher, is keen to develop the children's knowledge and understanding as well as their empathy with those living during the Tudor period, whilst also considering the opportunities and roles in society today.

Case Study: History focus

Aamir selects a historical novel by Mary Hooper entitled *At the House of the Magician*. He chooses to read this book aloud to the class, thus encouraging children's responses to the text as well as discussion of the content. Aamir decides that he will focus the learning activities linked to the book on English and history.

$\rightarrow$

He asks the children to write diary entries and letters, in role, to develop their understanding of the characters and thus empathise. He incorporates drama to stimulate the writing.

At the House of the Magician centres on the character of Lucy, who dreams of being a maid to gentry in the hope that she will get closer to Queen Elizabeth 1. Aamir and the children explore the role of women and the aspirations of the working classes during Tudor times. They also discuss employment opportunities and the currency and value of money at that time. They create job advertisements and write letters of application in the role of Lucy. In order to compare and contrast the historical periods, the children also create these for today's jobs.

Aamir focuses on historical details such as the court magician and consultants to the Queen, developing the children's understanding of how people lived in Tudor times. The children explore how key figures such as Sir Francis Walsingham and the Queen are presented throughout the novel and the literary devices that are employed to encourage reader empathy. Discussion also considers how accurate this fictional novel is and how accurate different accounts of history in general are likely to be and what might affect this.

The children in the case study above were enabled to gain an engaging perspective of history through literature and enjoy the story as it unfolded and presented historical details as well as developing fascinating and realistic characters to whom they could relate.

Links to the National Curriculum
The children in the case study are exploring authorial techniques. Alongside this, the children are exploring notions of character through dramatic techniques and how plot, narrative structure and themes are developed. Their writing tasks require them to use appropriate language and style.

The links to the NC for history are abundant as children are developing their chronological understanding. Their knowledge and understanding is developed as they are taught about characteristic features of the Elizabethan period and society. In exploring the accuracy of historical information, the children are understanding why historical events are represented and interpreted in different ways.

Text accuracy
Consideration should be given to the accuracy of the texts you present. In some cases it is preferable that accuracy should be ensured, for example to avoid misinformation about cultures or countries or the perpetuation of stereotypes. However, the following activity may initiate questions about how insistent you are on accurate portrayals and how, or indeed if, you use fiction to teach concepts.

Activity

Consider the popular picture book *The Very Hungry Caterpillar* by Eric Carle. In the story, a caterpillar eats a range of foods until its eventual metamorphosis into a beautiful butterfly. There are elements of factual representation of the life cycle of a butterfly, but some glaring inaccuracies that are purely fictional. Caterpillars do not eat sausages, cake, cheese or many of the other foods consumed and the life cycle itself is not fully explained.

Consider the following questions.

What is the purpose of sharing this book with children? How important is it that the story be scientifically accurate? Or is the sense of awe and wonder children gain from the book sufficient?

Would you use this story to teach the life cycle of a butterfly? Could you use it as a fictional representation and, if so, how? Are children enjoying *The Very Hungry Caterpillar* at an appropriate age to fully explore the life cycle of a butterfly?

How could this picture book be used, if at all, in relation to the life cycle of a butterfly? Would you present it to children without making mention of the science involved, purely as a picture book or story? Or is there a danger of children becoming confused by concepts and misunderstanding the life cycle of a butterfly as a result?

Would it be appropriate to enjoy this book first with children and then discuss and clarify the concepts? Or could this be detrimental to the enjoyment of the book? Is it necessary to treat every book as fact or truth and to explain to children when it is not? Would this create an issue with all works of fiction? Will fictional representation render much of literature 'inaccurate' and how important is this in sharing it with children? By its very nature, does literature present perspectives that are open to interpretation and contradiction?

What place does the imagination have in enjoying literature?

How far is it appropriate to teach important concepts through literature? Can literature be relied upon to do this? Can it act as a stimulus for discussion rather than direct teaching?

Can you think of any other children's books which might raise a similar conundrum to *The Very Hungry Caterpillar*?

How you use literature to 'teach' in a cross-curricular manner needs careful consideration, as this activity demonstrates. Certainly literature cannot take the place of clear and explicit teaching, but perhaps can be used to support or reinforce it. It is important to rely not on the literature but on your own secure subject knowledge to discern which texts to use and how to use them. It is generally insufficient to teach through the texts entirely; rather they can enhance teaching and learning and serve as motivating and exciting resources.

Another area to consider before embarking on using literature in a cross-curricular way is how this will be approached.

Approaches to using cross-curricular literature

Activity

Now that you have finished reading this chapter, revisit the types of curriculum explored in Chapter 1 and your own experiences of these. Consider the potential of each to incorporate literature to support learning across the curriculum. Some ideas are included in the table below, but you may have more of your own.

Curriculum model	Positives of using literature in cross-curricular manner	Drawbacks of using literature in cross-curricular manner	Your observations/comments
Subject specific approach (separate subject coverage)	Enlivens lesson. Provides opportunity to develop English skills alongside any subject	May not be current practice, so may be some resistance from staff or resourcing issues to overcome	
Creative curriculum; themed approach	Lends itself naturally to using literature in this way. Opportunities for creativity. Children accustomed to working this way. Links easily made	Neglecting focus on high quality literature to ensure merely that which 'fits' with topic	
Spiral curriculum	Opportunity to use literature to revisit and deepen learning. Can present themes in different ways through books	Difficulty in finding many texts to deepen learning through multiple exposures	

Table 3.1 Using texts to achieve cross-curricular aims

As suggested in Table 3.1 above, texts can be used in different ways to achieve cross-curricular aims. As well as considering the curriculum model you are working within, you will need to decide your starting point. This need not be consistent; different approaches may be appropriate on different occasions. However, you will need to be prepared for and knowledgeable about the advantages and disadvantages of different starting points in order to select the most effective.

Copy and complete Table 3.2 below to help you to investigate the pros and cons of using texts in different ways.

Starting point	Positives of this approach	Drawbacks of this approach	Other comments
Starting with a text and planning the learning around it			How is the text chosen? Do children input into this decision? Is whole school planning considered so that the same texts are not repeatedly used?
Starting with a topic and finding texts to support the learning			

Table 3.2 The pros and cons of using texts in different ways

As this activity suggests, whichever approach is taken towards using literature to support cross-curricular learning, careful consideration should be given to planning and to the ethos of teaching and learning. There are numerous benefits, but it is prudent to be aware of and prepared for potential challenges also.

Learning Outcomes Review

This chapter has explored the potential of children's literature to ignite or enhance cross-curricular learning. The case studies have presented several texts which could be used and outlined how they were used and the NC links that were made across the curriculum. The possibilities inherent within quality literature have been mentioned and some practical examples provided to support your planning and teaching.

Self-assessment questions
1. How can you begin to make cross-curricular links using literature?
2. Suggest two reasons why exploring children's literature can be beneficial.
3. Consider the books outlined in the case studies. Can you think of any other links across the curriculum that could be made using these texts? Are there any activities you would have planned differently?
4. List five children's books that you know and make notes on how they could be utilised to develop learning across the curriculum.

> 5. Explore children's bookshops and libraries to enhance your knowledge of children's literature.

Further Reading

It is important that you familiarise yourself with the different genres of fiction in order to present a broad, balanced and rich variety of literature to the children you teach. The following suggestions will enable you to read more about different genres as well as developing your understanding of the importance of literature and a positive ethos.

Gamble, N. and Yates, S. (2008) *Exploring Children's Literature* (2nd edition). London: SAGE.

Goodwin, P. (2008) *Understanding Children's Books; A guide for education professionals*. London: Sage.

In order to become familiar with children's literature, there is no substitute for browsing libraries and bookshops and generally exploring. You can also seek advice and recommendations from other teachers, parents and, of course, from children themselves. A useful resource is *The Core Booklist*, published by the Centre for Literacy in Primary Education (CLPE, 2010) and updated every two years. This presents a list of quality texts and a short blurb about each.

Similarly, Nicholas Tucker's *Rough Guide to Children's Books 5–11* (Rough Guide Ltd, 2002) is a starting point for researching authors and popular texts, but be aware that a multitude of children's books have become available since its publication. Keith Topping's research into the reading habits of 150,000 children in the UK may also be of interest to you (*What Kids are Reading*, published by Renaissance Learning, 2011).

Tucker's work on children's responses to literature is also helpful; *The Child and the Book: a psychological and literary exploration* (Cambridge University Press, 1981).

You are advised to read more about cross-curricular teaching. A good starting point for this is the work of Jonathon Barnes. In particular, his publication *Cross-curricular Learning 3–14* (2007) provides some excellent ideas as well as the theory behind the practice. To develop your understanding of cross-curricular approaches, you could also read David Wray's *Teaching Literacy Across the Primary Curriculum* (2006) and Trevor Kerry's *Cross-Curricular Teaching in the Primary School: Planning and facilitating imaginative lessons* (2011).

References

Barnes, J. (2007) *Cross-curricular Learning 3–14*. London: SAGE.

Chambers, A. (1986) *Book Talk, Occasional writing on literature and children*. UK: Harper Collins.

Chambers, A. (1995) *The Reading Environment*. UK: Stenhouse.

Corbett, P. (2008) *JumpStart Story Making Games and activities for ages 7–12.* UK: David Fulton.

Cremin, T., Mottram, M., Bearne, E. and Goodwin, P. (2008) Exploring teachers' knowledge of children's literature, *Cambridge Journal of Education*, 38(4), pp449–464.

Czerniewska, P. (1992) *Learning About Writing.* Oxford: Blackwell.

Dawes, L. and Birrell, S. (2000) In Grugeon, E., Dawes, L., Smith, C. and Hubbard, L. *Teaching Speaking and Listening in the Primary School* (3rd edition). Oxford: David Fulton.

Department for Education and Employment (DfEE) (1999) *The National Curriculum handbook for primary teachers in England in key stages 1 and 2.* London: The Stationery Office.

Fox, C. (1992) In Harrison, C. and Coles, M. *The Reading for Real Handbook.* London: Routledge.

Goodwin, P. (2008) *Understanding Children's Books; A guide for education professionals.* London: Sage.

Meek, M. (1982) *Learning to Read.* London: Bodley Head.

Meek, M. (1988) *How Texts Teach What Readers Learn.* UK: Thimble Press.

Palmer, S. (2011) *Speaking Frames, How to Teach Talk for Writing.* Oxford: Routledge.

Smith, F. (1985) *Reading.* Cambridge: Cambridge University Press.

Wray, D. (2006) *Teaching Literacy across the Primary Curriculum.* Exeter: Learning Matters.

4. Non-fiction text types

Learning Outcomes

This chapter aims to help you to:

- recognise the challenges that non-fiction reading and writing present to primary-aged children;
- become familiar with the language and layout features of a range of non-fiction text types;
- reflect on how boys' interest in information texts can be used to develop their learning in literacy and across the curriculum;
- consider ways to engage children in reading and writing information texts through incorporating creative cross curricular approaches.

TEACHERS' STANDARDS

A teacher must:

1. Set high expectations which inspire, motivate and challenge pupils

- set goals that stretch and challenge pupils of all backgrounds, abilities and dispositions

2. Promote good progress and outcomes by pupils

- plan teaching to build on pupils' capabilities and prior knowledge
- encourage pupils to take a responsible and conscientious attitude to their own work and study

3. Demonstrate good subject and curriculum knowledge

- have a secure knowledge of the relevant subject(s) and curriculum areas; foster and maintain pupils' interest in the subject
- promote the value of scholarship

4. Plan and teach well structured lessons

- promote a love of learning and children's intellectual curiosity
- contribute to the design and provision of an engaging curriculum within the relevant subject area(s)

5. Adapt teaching to respond to the strengths and needs of all pupils

- have a secure understanding of how a range of factors can inhibit pupils' ability to learn, and how best to overcome these

Introduction

This chapter focuses on developing your knowledge of different non-fiction text types and how you can use this knowledge to develop children's speaking and listening, reading and writing skills across a range of National Curriculum subjects. You will also be introduced to strategies that will enable your teaching and children's learning of non-fiction to be both creative and stimulating.

The importance of non-fiction

Non-fiction texts are significant as they provide different types of information which will enable children to access curriculum subjects and acquire essential knowledge, explore pertinent ideas and gain a greater understanding of how literacy can be used to serve important functions in their everyday lives (Graves, 1994). In our highly technologically-dependent society, reading and writing for a range of purposes – using a diverse variety of communication media – continues to grow in importance and relevance.

Over the past few days, have you glanced at a newspaper or magazine article, composed an email, examined a timetable, sent a text message to a friend, addressed an envelope, flicked through a holiday brochure, read the nutrition information on a food packet, accessed information through a search engine or scribbled down a shopping list?

All of these are everyday examples of different types of non-fiction reading and writing. Many people enjoy reading and listening to stories, plays and poetry, and we should never dismiss their importance as an effective means of helping us to communicate with others. They also allow us to recognise universal truths, give us insights into our own culture and practices and those of others and, in terms of formal education, they help us to gain literacy knowledge and attainment. However, as exemplified above, it is non-fiction reading and writing which constitutes the majority of functional literacy tasks that most adults will undertake as part of their employment, cultural or social experience.

When teachers are clear about the audiences for, and purposes of, different forms of non-fiction reading and writing, they will be able to prepare their pupils for the literacy opportunities and challenges that they will face both within school and as part of their adult lives. Therefore, it is important that the complexities and fulfilment of reading and writing in relation to the wide range of available non-fiction texts is made clear to those who will be teaching primary age children.

Non-fiction versus fiction

In order to avoid possible confusion and overlap when different text types or genres are discussed it is important to establish the difference between the terms *non-fiction* and *fiction*.

Non-fiction deals with factual (or assumed factual) events, explanations, descriptions, opinions and observations. It can be used both to gain and challenge knowledge and information – consider the use of hard copy and online encyclopaedias, atlases and thesauri – and also to develop recognition of the different ways that specific ideas and phenomena are communicated. Non-fiction is complex to classify as it contains a diverse range of texts which are used in a range of ways which can serve different educational and social purposes. Libraries in Britain and worldwide that use the Dewey Decimal Classification system attempt to overcome this by organising books through subject categorisation and subdivision using decimal numerical notation. However, this type of cataloguing does not necessarily encompass different non book-based varieties of non-fiction such as letters, advertisements and posters.

In contrast, fiction is a description of any narrative or informative work that deals with portraying imaginary information or events. Most stories, play scripts and poems would be considered works of fiction if they are built around imagined characters, settings, situations and themes. Fiction, which can be categorised into different types or genres, for example, traditional tales, science fiction or comic verse, whose main aim is to entertain and provide enjoyment, is recognised, through the Dewey Decimal Classification library system and the National Curriculum's English Programmes of Study, as 'literature'. Chapter 3 has already examined how such texts could be used in your classroom in a cross-curricular manner.

Challenges: non-fiction reading

Children need to learn to read accurately and to understand how the written word can be organised as the knowledge and understanding of vocabulary, grammar, punctuation and text structures that they gain from reading underpins the knowledge and skills that they bring to their written work. To be able to do this, they rely upon a range of strategies to enable them to decode the words on the page as well as to comprehend the meanings of unfamiliar words and texts. By nature of their factual content, structure and language, non-fiction texts pose more difficulties for readers than fiction. The following activity will go some way to illustrating the problems that some non-fiction reading can present to even the most able reader.

Activity

Copy the two cloze passages below, A and B, by inserting appropriate words so that the extracts make sense. Can you identify the non-fiction text types that you are reading?

A.

I _____ through the lens as John _____ ankle deep in the waves, looking out to sea. _____ was his first swim in _____ years. It seemed such _____ perfect expression of _____ and _____ was happy to be sharing it with him. I watched as he _____to stare out towards the _____. He looked exactly the same. The photograph I _____, when it _____ developed, could _____ from any one of our holidays six, seven years _____. But, after all that had _____ since then, there was so much to learn about each other, _____ much to understand about that _____ time.

> **B.**
> A yellow, green, or brown _____ fluid _____ by the liver and _____
> in the gall bladder. _____ of the gall bladder, _____ is triggered by a
> _____ that is released from the _____ in the _____ of food, causes
> the bile to be expelled through the _____ bile duct into the intestine.
> _____ is composed of a mixture of bile salts (which _____ fatty food for
> digestion) and _____ (a breakdown product of the blood _____
> haemoglobin).

Which extract did you find easier to complete? Check your word preferences against the completed passages below. How accurate were your choices?

A. I <u>watched</u> through the lens as John <u>stood</u> ankle deep in the waves, looking out to sea. <u>It</u> was his first swim in <u>six</u> years. It seemed such <u>a</u> perfect expression of <u>freedom</u> and <u>I</u> was happy to be sharing it with him. I watched as he <u>continued</u> to stare out towards the <u>horizon</u>. He looked exactly the same. The photograph I <u>took</u>, when it <u>was</u> developed, could <u>be</u> from any one of our holidays six, seven years <u>before</u>. But, after all that had <u>happened</u> since then, there was so much to learn about each other, <u>so</u> much to understand about that <u>stolen</u> time. *Published by Bantam Press entitled Some Other Rainbow and written by John McCarthy and Jill Morrell.*

B. A yellow, green, or brown <u>alkaline</u> fluid <u>secreted</u> by the liver and <u>stored</u> in the gall bladder. <u>Contraction</u> of the gall bladder, <u>which</u> is triggered by a <u>hormone</u> that is released from the <u>duodenum</u> in the <u>presence</u> of food, causes the bile to be expelled through the <u>common</u> bile duct into the intestine. Bile is composed of a mixture of bile salts (which <u>emulsify</u> fatty food for digestion) and <u>bilirubin</u> (a breakdown product of the blood <u>pigment</u> haemoglobin).

Unless you are an expert on the human digestive system, you probably found it easier to make sense of A, which is a factual narrative or recount, and that the words that you choose for the first extract were close in meaning to the original author's writing. At times, there were only a number of options that you could have inserted. For example, what would you do 'through a lens' other than to look, peer, squint or stare? In this instance, you sought out a verb that related in some way to 'looking'. If you were successful in completing this passage, it is because you wanted the sentences to 'make sense' and drew on your knowledge of syntactical, grammatical awareness as well as particular, familiar contexts. Familiarity with the language of narrative texts also helped you to anticipate words before they appeared in the extract.

A science encyclopaedia extract such as B, while not being any more difficult to decode in respect of reading the words on the page, would have been much more complicated for you to complete. You may have struggled to fill some gaps as locating the exact, specific scientific terms is more problematic unless you already have expert knowledge of the subject.

We draw on reading 'cues' or strategies to help us to comprehend the meanings contained within texts. We may be able to use our phonemic awareness to 'sound out' unfamiliar words or recognise words by their visual similarity or analogy with words that we can already read but it does not necessarily follow that we understand what these newly decoded words mean. Within non-fiction texts, there are often more new nouns to process that may never have been seen or heard before. Some nouns are only encountered when reading about a particular discipline or subject. When would you come across the words *sarcophagus* or *mummification* unless within the context of an ancient civilisation burial ritual or *precipitation* and *meteorologists* except in a discussion related to the weather? If unfamiliar words do not have a synonymic equivalent, that is words that have a close, or similar, meaning, then it is not easy to insert a substitute. Word processor synonym checkers offer no suggestions for *alkali* just as they do not give a suggestion for *giraffe* so it is hard for readers to draw on contextual knowledge that is not there!

Activity

To illustrate this further and lead into the next considerations about non-fiction reading, see how easy it is for you to make the meanings of words clear. Can you clearly define the following words in statements of 6 words or fewer as per the example that has been given?

Example: secret - hidden from knowledge or view

territorial	surprise	auction	book	green
badger	measure	swim	table	brush

Did you notice that some of the words in the activity have a number of meanings as they can act as verbs, nouns, and even adjectives depending on the context in which they appear in writing? Which word class did you choose to define, and why?

Language challenges

To ensure that the meanings of new words are clear to readers, authors of non-fiction often need to include a range of language devices to clarify meaning. This can include placing additional information into a sentence through additional, adjunctive or embedded phrases. For example, in the following sentence the unlined words are an example of a complex subject noun phras: *'The remains and shapes of animals and plants buried for millions of years in the earth's rocks are called fossils'*. The explanation incorporated into the phrase helps to clarify meaning of the unfamiliar word 'fossil' but involves more extensive 'reading'. Sometimes, words and phrases are needed between the subject and the verb, such as in this sentence: 'The *agouti*, a very nervous 40cm, 3kg rodent from South America, can leap twenty feet from a sitting position'. Here the additional, underlined information has been included to enable a greater understanding of the unfamiliar subject under discussion.

There may also be an over-reliance on different types of clauses such as those that relate information: *'Tiger species that are in danger need protection.'* (defining relative clause) or those that concede possible debate: *'Although whales are in danger, they are still hunted and killed' (concessional clause).* It may be that a clause is inserted or joined to a main sentence or clause to give reasons: *'Due to deforestation, the Giant Panda has been driven out of the lowland areas where it once lived.' (subordinate clause).* All of this additional language has to be read and understood for the subject within the non-fiction text to come alive to the reader with positive outcomes being the child's development of a richer, specialised vocabulary and knowledge of advanced syntactic structures (Mallett, 2010).

Structural challenges

Authors and publishers of non-fiction not only use language devices to help a reader to navigate through the written information within the text; considerable time is spent on deciding where to include layout features such as titles, subheadings and bullet points. Drawings, photographs or diagrams, that are matched through the use of captions or close proximity to the paragraphs that they are meant to illustrate, might also be used; they help with comprehension of word meanings and subject matter and so make the text more appealing and accessible, especially to visual learners. Glossaries or mini dictionaries and indexes, which require accurate alphabetic knowledge to enable navigation, might also be included in non-fiction reference books as will content lists. Many of these features have become accepted conventions that define a specific form of non-fiction writing.

Activity

Choose a children's non-fiction book or website on a subject with which you are unfamiliar. Read a few pages or follow a number of hyperlinks and examine how the author tries to organise the information for the reader. How clear is the language within the text? What layout devices are employed and how successful do you deem them to be? Could the author have developed the text differently on the page to make it easier to read or understand?

Links to the National Curriculum

It is important that children are taught to read for meaning using grammatical awareness and contextual understanding. Children also need to be taught to recognise and use organisational features and systems to find information in non-fiction texts. It is essential to ensure a breadth of study within the National Curriculum and use a range of sources of information in all curriculum subjects.

Choosing non-fiction texts for the classroom

Certain types of non-fiction could be said to be easily recognised by the 'facts' on which they are focused. Others are distinguished by the way in which they are conventionally laid out or formatted such as newspapers (headlines, columns, short paragraphs), posters (different sized fonts, font styles, colour, text and graphics organisation) and letters (address, date, greeting, message, signature). Many recently published texts, in their attempts to motivate readers, will incorporate different types of fiction and non-fiction writing. An example of this would be a magazine-style children's comic which, together with comic strip stories, may contain articles, reports, advertisements, letters to the editor and recipes or instructions.

As mentioned in Chapter 3, it is imperative that primary classrooms contain a range of good quality fiction to enthuse children to becoming passionate, analytical and discerning readers. It is also important for teachers to provide children with adequate access to a variety of non-fiction texts which can be used to develop their language and reading skills, increase their knowledge of the world around them and help to prepare them for a range of reading and writing tasks that they may encounter. Many popular progressive reading 'schemes' such as Rigby Star (Pearson), Kingscourt (McGraw/Hill) and Alphakids (Gardner Education) include collections of good, quality non-fiction texts. As a class teacher, you need to ensure that you collect enough books on the curriculum areas or subjects that you will be introducing to children so that they can access material to support their interests and which are at their reading level. While books would form the bulk of non-fiction material that is made available in classrooms or school libraries, magazines, newspapers, comics, leaflets, brochures, catalogues and posters – as well as screen-based media such as interactive websites – could all be included in the non-fiction 'diet' that is delivered to children which will help them to develop their reading skills and knowledge.

Challenges: non-fiction writing

While we have focused on some of the challenges of non-fiction reading, some of these also transfer to writing as children attempt to replicate or reproduce a text type to write in particular, socially-accepted format. The differences that define each non-fiction text type, which will be explored later in the chapter, introduce children to the available range of the written word but also present challenges for the young writer, whatever their stage of writing development.

Children need to get to know the established 'rules' that should be applied when writing non-fiction and to do this you need to:

- familiarise children with the text type;
- focus children's attention on the key features;
- define the conventions of the genre;
- support children to use the text type.

Explicit literacy lessons where you systematically introduce, model (demonstrate using a 'doing and thinking aloud' strategy) and reinforce the different knowledge and skills needed for writing are essential and need to be well planned. Included in planning should be engaging opportunities for speaking and listening, group discussion and drama. Getting an appropriate balance of whole class modelled and shared writing with guided group work to scaffold writing within lessons should be the aim of all trainees and teachers to ensure that children develop the confidence and skills to become independent writers.

Case Study: Citizenship

Michelle is completing a placement within a Year 5 class and wants to introduce the children to influential campaigners and people who have had a positive impact on our world. The school has embarked on a Personal, Social and Health Education (PHSE) topic of 'Heroes' and wanted children to appreciate enduring heroic endeavour rather than the fleeting celebrity status of footballers and pop stars. The teachers in Upper Key Stage 2 selected David A. Alder's *Picture Book Biography Series* as a useful resource for examining non-fiction recounts of the lives of famous people.

Within this series, Michelle decides to start with *A Picture Book of Rosa Parks* which explored the life of an Afro-American civil rights activist. She reads the story to the children and stops at regular intervals for discussion and for children to clarify events and issues and relate these to their own worlds and experiences. The discussion is particularly emotive and the children are inspired by Rosa's bravery and commitment. They are able to understand in human terms the Civil Rights Movement in America and are shocked by how recently racial segregation was legal and accepted.

The children dramatise the story in small groups and then perform to each other. Their understanding of the events is exceptional and enhanced by the chance to discuss and undertake role play. They then think of modern day examples of discrimination or unfairness which they dramatise. Michelle models sensitivity towards children's responses and their experiences.

Additional learning involves diary writing in role, digitally recording news reports and creating posters that campaigned on behalf of Rosa Parks. The children also write and then film their readings of acceptance speeches Rosa might have made for the numerous awards and medals she received. The children are also asked to write a recount of the story of Rosa and to produce timelines of events around that period. Some of the oral and drama work that the children carry out is shown in the whole school 'Heroes' assembly and their posters form part of the 'Heroes' display in the school's entrance lobby.

Links to the National Curriculum

At the time of writing, Citizenship was recommended to be reclassified as a part of the Basic Curriculum from Key Stage 3 in England (DfE, 2011). However, National Curriculum guidance suggests that children in Key Stage 2 should develop their sense of social justice and moral responsibility and schools continue to teach PSHE.

> Through group discussion and role play children develop their speaking and listening skills. The broadcasting and writing activities aim for children to recognise and use writing for different purposes through using a range of writing activities.

Non-fiction genres

The previous chapter explained that children's fiction can be divided into specific genres, for example, traditional tales, fables, science fiction and mystery stories. This is also true of non-fiction as there is a range a text types that have been identified following the work of a number of Australian genre theorists who explored how non-fiction can be distinguished by its subject, language and form and how it could be taught (for an overview see Reid, 1987). As an illustration, let us briefly consider some of the differences between science fiction stories and traditional tales before we focus on the distinctions between non-fiction text types. This should help to focus your attention on how knowledge of both the layout or structure and the language used in texts is essential to developing an overall, and specific, understanding of the material that it contains.

Science fiction is recognised as being speculative as it often contains highly descriptive, imaginary or futuristic 'worlds' which are inhabited by unfamiliar 'aliens'. Scientific or technological language is employed in the fast pace of unfolding events where the emphasis on the plot line is stronger than the development of the characters. In contrast, traditional tales are based on an oral tradition of storytelling which served a social purpose of attempting to influence behaviour and unite people within cultures. The plots are simple, full of formulaic language and are often based on defeating a real or metaphorical 'monster' or overcoming adversity through the use of stereotypical characters. These are clear examples of how variations in structure features and language help to support understanding of the particular genres.

While there are some (Barrs, 1987; Bearne et al, 2004 cited in Mallett 2010) who would question the 'genre theory' classification in relation to non-fiction reading and writing, the non-statutory National Literacy Strategy and Primary National Strategy Frameworks for Literacy (DfEE 1998; DfES 2006), which some primary schools use, developed the demands of the statutory curriculum by promoting the explicit teaching of different non -fiction text types. Listed below are the six non-fiction genres or text types that are typically focussed upon in primary schools.

1. Recounts

2. Non-chronological reports

3. Instructions or procedures

4. Persuasion texts

5. Explanatory texts

6. Discussion texts

As with all effective literacy, or indeed, educational practice, any focus on the teaching and learning of non-fiction should be at a level that children are able to understand and within a context that they would find familiar and meaningful. It should incorporate opportunities for children to make links between their oral literacy and reading and writing experiences and, as such, suits both a subject specific and a cross-curricular approach. Through other subject disciplines as well as cross-curricular approaches, children can further explore and apply the subtleties of spoken and written language and build on their literacy lessons.

The following descriptions of the different types of texts are based upon, and adapted from, the information provided by the Primary Strategies which disseminated guidance and information to primary schools through its various published and online resources. Some short examples of how the text types can be used within other subject areas have been added.

Recounts are sometimes referred to as 'accounts'. They are the most common text type that readers and listeners encounter, not least because they are the basic form of many factual storytelling texts. In non-fiction texts, they are used to provide an accurate account of events.

Generic structure	Language features
Title gives subject of recount.	Mostly written in the past tense.
Events stated in time or chronological order. Includes key facts – who, what, where, when and why?	Focused on individual characters and /or single or sequential events. Time connectives used.

Table 4.1 Recounts

Cross-curricular examples: History: biographies, diary entries, and autobiographies of historical figures (scientists, inventors, politicians, saints, social reformers, artists, musicians, monarchs). Science: recounting tests on a range of everyday materials. Geography: newspaper reports on a topical national or international weather event.

Non-chronological reports describe things the way they are, so they usually present information in an objective way. The writing is organised without reference to a sequence of events – it is not time ordered – and would be typically organised by characteristics and attributes.

Generic text structure	Language features
A general opening that classifies.	Often written in the third person.
A description of the phenomenon that includes qualities, parts, functions, habits and behaviour.	Usually written in the present tense but may be written in the past tense within a historical report.
	Tends to focus on generic subjects rather than specific subjects.
	Description is generally used for precision rather than to create an emotional response.

Table 4.2 Non-chronological reports

Cross-curricular examples: Music: creating a class dictionary which explains useful musical vocabulary, signs and symbols. History: leaflet guides to places of local interest or an encyclopaedia describing images of Ancient Egyptian/Greek artefacts held in the British Museum.

Instructional texts describe or instruct how something is done through a series of steps.

Generic text structure	Language features
Instructional texts include an initial title which explains the goal of the instructions. List of materials. Sequence of steps. Diagrams or illustrations included.	Steps written in chronological order. Steps written using imperative verbs. Focus on generalised human agents rather than named individuals.

Table 4.3 Instructional texts

Cross-curricular examples: Design and Technology: recipes for healthy snacks and drinks. ICT: 'How to. . .' guide for programming a floor turtle.

Explanatory texts focus on explaining about the 'how' and 'why' of natural and man made objects and phenomena such as how something works or happened. They often go beyond simple description or instruction as they include information about causes, motives or reasons.

Generic text structure	Language features
A general statement to introduce the topic. A series of logical steps to explain how or why something occurs which continue until the final state is shown.	Usually written in the simple present tense. Includes connectives that signal time, e.g. *then, after that, finally.* Causal connectives are incorporated, e.g. *so, because of this.* Specialised terminology.

Table 4.4 Explanatory texts

Cross-curriculat examples: Science: a poster explaining plant pollination. History: an illustrated timeline exploring the lives and fates of the wives of Henry VIII.

Discussion texts present a balanced 'for and against' argument. They usually aim to provide two or more different views on an issue idea, each with elaborations, evidence and/or examples.

Generic text structure	Language features
Statement of the issue plus a preview of the main arguments.	Written in the simple present tense and third person.
Arguments for and then against, plus supporting evidence. These may be alternated in the main body.	Contains generic human or non-human participants.
	Uses logical connectives.
Summary and conclusion which balances the evidence.	Moves from general to the specific.

Table 4.5 Discussion texts

Cross-curricular examples: PHSE: debate a topical school issue (bullying/ friendship/school dinners). History: consider the advantages/ disadvantages of child evacuation during the Second World War. Geography: study of a local land use issue.

Persuasive texts attempt to argue a case for a particular point of view. Their purpose is to attempt to convince or persuade a reader to share the opinions expressed.

Generic text structure	Language features
Statement of point of view.	Written in the simple present tense.
Arguments.	Focus on generic participants rather than particular ones.
Reiteration, summary and re-statement of the original position.	Contains logical connectives, not generally time connectives.
	Paragraph connectives.
	Emotive language employed.
	Use of rhetorical questions.
	General to the specific.

Table 4.6 Persuasive texts

Cross-curricular examples: Geography: creating a tourist brochure for a less economically-developed country. Art and Design: devising advertisements for a forthcoming school fund-raising event. Mathematics: using data to support arguments.

Activity

From the genre descriptions above, can you match the non-fiction text type to the description of writing?

Text type	Writing
A instruction	1. an encyclopaedia entry about humped back whales
B persuasion	2. a poster about the journey of a river
C recount	3. a recipe for chocolate refrigerator cake
D non-chronological report	4. a letter asking for a football season ticket refund
E explanation	5. the transcript of a radio debate on climate change
F discussion	6. a magazine article about a recent Amazonian jungle exploration

Table 4.7 Matching text types

The answers are given at the end of the chapter on page 76.

Boys and non-fiction

Studies and government data shows us that girls perform better than boys in attaining higher levels of literacy, with the most recent Programme for International Student Assessment (PISA) analysis identifying that more girls than boys in economically developed countries read for enjoyment (OECD, 2011). Only 38 per cent of boys in the UK enjoy writing for family, friends or school compared to 52 per cent of girls (National Literacy Trust 2010; 2011). Smith and Wilhelm (2002) highlighted the preference of boys for non-fiction and visual texts which can be a useful starting point for many teachers if they recognise and use the knowledge of gender preferences when planning lesson activities. While it would be unwise to pander to boys' inclination to read only factual books or comics at the expense of their overall literacy development, awareness of how many boys prefer physically interactive activities, and technologically-based reading and writing can help in devising cross-curricular literacy-based activities.

Research Focus: Curiosity Kits

In an attempt to engage a greater number of Year 3 and 4 boys in reading, a country-wide pilot project developed by Maureen Lewis and Ros Fisher of the University of Exeter, for the United Kingdom Reading Association, was launched during the 1999 Year of Reading. Intended to capture the interest of reluctant and struggling boy readers, Curiosity Kits were sports bags that contained:

- a non-fiction book;
- a related toy or artefact;
- a wipe clean, word search related to the book;

→

- a wipe clean, design activity;
- a magazine on the same topic as the non-fiction book, aimed at adults;
- comment stickers and a comment book.

The kits were devised to be shared by parents and children – especially fathers – at home and would be based on male preference topics such as reptiles, bikes, space, machines and different sports. The aim of the project was twofold; to counteract the idea of the idea of reading as a feminine activity by highlighting the male sharing aspect and to rekindle the interest in reading that often flags in boys within lower Key Stage 2.

Research findings into the initial use of the kits found that more positive attitudes towards reading were developed as boys read more with fathers, grandfathers and other male family members at home and levels of enthusiasm for reading increased in those schools that utilised the kits.

Many schools have since taken up and expanded upon the ideas of the original project and found that reading motivation has improved. Children become more familiar with subject based, non-fiction texts which inspire purposeful discussion and support reading, writing and research skills both at home and within school.

Research skills

While Mallett (2010) would contend that using non-fiction *just* to develop study skills is not the most effective model, it is important for teachers to consider in which ways non-fiction texts can be used to develop children's research capabilities. Children need to learn to:

- establish existing knowledge and specific areas for research;
- locate reference material;
- navigate alphabetically ordered materials;
- locate information within an identified paragraph/ page of a book or screen-based text;
- make notes;
- evaluate reference material.

You will be using these skills in your own research (see Chapter 8) and you will need to model and share these with children, based on your school's curriculum model.

Wray and Lewis (1997) devised a systematic way of developing these literacy research skills called the EXIT (Extending Interactions with Texts) model. Simplified, it states that children need to:

- make connections to what they already know;
- have a purpose for seeking information;

- know *where* and *how* to find appropriate information;
- understand what they read and make it their own;
- make a record of the information they find;
- evaluate it for accuracy or bias;
- choose an appropriate means to communicate the information.

Once children have grasped these skills, they should be given plenty of opportunities to practise these in a range of contexts in other discrete subjects or through a cross-curricular approach. The following case study shows how a trainee teacher built on children's interests to develop their enquiry and research skills in a creative manner.

Case Study: Combining skills in core subjects

Zack, a third year student, is on his final placement in a school which follows a theme-based curriculum. The core subjects of English and mathematics are systematically planned to be incorporated with the remaining curriculum subjects so that there was a clear progression of literacy and mathematical skills development. The school is keen for all children to develop their independent enquiry skills but, following the recommendations from their recent Ofsted inspection, is working towards developing the children's writing so that it is more purposeful and imaginative and not just simply a means of recording what the children had learnt.

Based in a Year 3 class, Zack is enthusiastic to learn that the school's extensive outdoor area which includes a large sports field, ponds and woodlands could be utilised for his year group's science-based 'Minibeasts' topic. This gives him plenty of scope to devise a range of practical activities which involve the children investigating different animal habitats and searching for creatures that live in them.

Once a range of minibeasts is collected, observed and classified through different scientific investigations, including finding out which type and colour of food that slugs and snails preferred and how quickly worms could help to decompose waste food matter, Zack is keen for children to consolidate and enlarge their scientific knowledge of adaptation and feeding relationships through additional text-based research. He sees this is as an ideal opportunity for most of the children to consolidate their higher order reading skills of skimming and scanning and to develop their ability to use organisational devices such as contents and index pages and glossaries to locate specific information quickly and accurately.

Recognising that there was a range of reading abilities within the class, Zack assembles books and extracts from other formats to support the children to carry out note-taking activities and table/ chart completion tasks in ability groups.

$\rightarrow$

He sets up a carousel of different reading activities around the classroom where children collect information to enhance their knowledge of insects and other minibeasts such as butterflies, ladybirds, beetles, worms and woodlice.

The Little Nippers Creepy Creatures series of non-chronological report style books published by Heinneman is an easily accessible resource with clear illustrations and clear text to engage the lower ability children's interest while Usbourne Pocket Nature books are more suitable for the more able readers.

A bank of laptops is set up with children instructed to link to a number of different websites including www.uksafari.com and www.ypte.org.uk/animal-facts.php

Another table contains enlarged pictures and posters of minibeasts and magnifiers so that the children could observe, discuss and explore the number of legs, body parts and antenna of animals that they may not have been able to find in the school grounds as Zack is very aware of the importance of group discussion in consolidating learning and gaining additional knowledge.

Although they are familiar with the organisational devices of titles, subheadings and captions which would help the children access information, Zack has already ensured that the children are able to navigate around the alphabetically ordered index pages of the books by giving the children many short, dictionary-based tasks which have also helped to improve their spelling and vocabulary.

From their notes and completed charts, the children compile fact files which cover a range of different fields such as the colour, length, habitat, diets and habits of six 'minibeasts' of their choice. Some children input the data onto a computerised database which helps to develop their ICT skills of saving work and data retrieval.

However, to engage the children further and to support the school's creative writing impetus, Zack concentrates his follow-on literacy linked planning and teaching on attaining a writing outcome for the children to be able to read, write and solve poetic riddles. This is based on using the information that they had collected about a range of common insects, worms, crustaceans and molluscs but would be rewritten in a different, creative form. Zack also plans a follow-on mathematics linked plan related to data analysis.

To ensure that the children are aware of the structure of riddles, Zack carries out some modelled reading of this poetry text type focusing on the figurative language that it usually employed. He then encourages the children to use their 'facts' to help them when constructing their own riddles. Here is an example of work from Zack's class:

→

Snakelike, slithering under the ground

Ploughing like a farmer and hiding from the bird's eye

I breathe through my slimy skin

Eating leaves and dirt

What am I?

A worm.

Links to the National Curriculum

As part of a science topic, children's observations and enquiries into living things in their environments are the main focus. A computerised database enables children to make effective use of ICT to save and retrieve information. Using and applying measurements practices children's mathematics skills. Reading for information using organisation features of texts and using the information that they had located allowed the children to address English programmes of study while their important group discussions and creative poetry writing encompassed speaking and listening and writing.

Communicating and presenting information

Written work in other areas of the curriculum can provide a meaningful context for the application of literacy skills. To help engage children, it is important to recognise the importance of creative teaching and learning approaches that help children to communicate their learning to others and learn from each other.

Primary-aged children are expected to present their work appropriately; selecting different tools confidently to match audience and purpose. It can challenge children's knowledge to communicate what they have learned in an unusual way, working towards a specific final product can be very motivating for children and can support the skills of editing and information selection. Work can be handwritten or word processed. We have found the following ideas to work well.

Individual or group displays: Not all final products have to be presented in individual books. Classroom displays capitalise on the benefits of audience and can be very stimulating, especially if children have some input into how the display will be produced. Display tasks can be allocated so that the whole class contribute to a comprehensive presentation of a topic.

'Mini' books: Production of 'mini' books – perhaps using one of the well known paper folding formats suggested through the work of Paul Johnson (2000) can work well for brief, self-contained topics. Onscreen 'e-books' where children develop their own interactive hyperlinks can link English and ICT effectively. All of these formats encourage children to be selective in the information they choose to include in their writing which helps develop their editing skills.

Television or radio broadcasts: Not all final products have to be in written form. There are a number of different hand-held devices that can be used for recording voices that even very young children can easily operate. Children can also make audio guides for museum visits which can be played back through computers using free, downloadable software such as Audacity: (http://audacity.sourceforge.net/)

Children can compose their own music using tuned/untuned percussion or digital musical software to accompany or embellish their spoken words.

Write a reference, explanation or instructional text for younger children: It is quite common for children in Key Stage 2 to write fiction books for younger children. The idea can also work well for non-fiction. Children will need to be very selective and to consider language and information very carefully to meet the needs of a younger audience.

Write a narrative to include information learned: Information acquired through art, religious education, science, history or geography-based topics might be turned into a narrative. Children will need to maintain key facts but might add characters and settings as appropriate. Reading books that could be used to model examples of this include Lawrence Anholt's Artist series or the Talking About my Faith series published by Franklin Watts.

Compile an encyclopaedia text: Information can be presented in a very straightforward alphabetical format. This can work well as a small group or whole class project in which individual children take responsibility for different entries.

Design an information leaflet: A4 paper, simply folded into three, makes a good leaflet format. This can be used for various topics, for instance, a geographical or historical guide to the local town or village or a visitor's guide to a museum written following a class trip. This makes a change from the usual recount writing which tends to include less about the delights of the museum and more of '*what I had in my lunch box and who was sick on the coach!*'

Compile a mail order or online catalogue: This works well for costume, jewellery, tools, weapons and household items in any period of history. Children can also apply what they know about the houses of a historical period to create an estate agent's 'blurb'.

Links to the National Curriculum

It is important that children use a wide range of methods to communicate and present observations. Children need to communicate in different ways which are appropriate to the task and audience.

Learning Outcomes Review

This chapter has encouraged you to consider how children need to gain the knowledge of the range of non-fiction texts before they can use them to search for information and create their own texts. It has shown how non-fiction can be used to support learning in literacy and other subjects in creative ways which can sustain the interests of all children, including boys.

Self-assessment questions
1. Which non-fiction material should be available in a primary classroom?
2. What are some of the challenges that non-fiction writing can present to primary-aged children?

Answers to activity on pages 69–70:
A:3   B:4   C:6   D:1   E:2   F:5

Further Reading

Lewis, M. and Fisher, R. (2003) *Curiosity Kits*. Reading: National Centre for Language and Literacy. This text gives further information about Curiosity Kits and how they can be set up in schools.

Seely, J. (2009) *Oxford A–Z of Grammar and Punctuation*. Oxford: Oxford University Press. If you find that some of the grammatical terms mentioned in this chapter are unfamiliar, this book will help to develop your subject knowledge.

www.gettingboystoread.com/content/getting-boys-read-quick-tips-parents-librarians-and-teachers accessed 15 January 2012. This website will give you some practical ideas for motivating reluctant boy readers and writers.

References

DfE (2011) *The Framework for the National Curriculum. A Report by the Expert Panel for the National Curriculum Review*. London: DfE.

DfEE (1998) *National Literacy Strategy – Framework For Literacy*. London: DfEE.

DfEE (1999) *The National Curriculum Handbook for Primary Teachers in England in Key Stages 1 and 2*. London: The Stationery Office.

DfES (2006) Primary National Strategy Frameworks for Literacy and Mathematics. London: DfES.

Graves, D. (1994) *A Fresh Look at Writing*. Portsmouth: Heinemann.

Johnson, P. (2000) *Making Books*. London: A & C Black.

Lewis, M. and Fisher, R. (2003) *Curiosity Kits*. Reading: National Centre for Language and Literacy.

Mallett, M. (2010) *Choosing and Using Fiction and Non-Fiction 3–11*. Abingdon: Routledge.

National Literacy Trust. *Young People's Reading and Writing Today 2010/2011* http://www.literacytrust.org.uk/assets/0001/0177/Attitudes_towards_Reading_Writing_Final_2011.pdf accessed 8 January 2012.

Programme for International Student Assessment http://www.pisa.oecd.org/dataoecd/34/50/48624701.pdf accessed 12 January 2012.

Reid, I. (ed) (1987) *The Place of Genre in Learning: current debates*. Victoria: Deakin University.

Smith, M.W. and Wilhelm, J.D. (2002) *Reading Don't Fix No Chevys: Literacy in the Lives of Young Men*. Portsmouth, NH: Heinemann.

Wray, D. (2006) *Teaching Literacy Across the Primary Curriculum*. Exeter: Learning Matters.

Wray, D. and Lewis, M. (1997) *Extending Literacy: Children reading and writing non-fiction*. London: Routledge.

5. English as an additional language

Learning Outcomes

This chapter aims to help you to:
- be able to describe some of the key terminology involved in EAL work;
- be able to describe the issues relating to cross-curricular teaching of EAL pupils in mainstream classroom;
- relate the key stages of EAL acquisition to cross-curricular teaching;
- relate the key principles of the teaching and learning of language to EAL pupils to a range of cross-curricular situations;
- be able to describe how support systems for EAL pupils and their teachers are utilised in cross-curricular teaching.

TEACHERS' STANDARDS

A teacher must:

1. **Set high expectations, which inspire, motivate and challenge pupils**
- establish a safe and stimulating environment for pupils, rooted in mutual respect
- set goals that stretch and challenge pupils of all backgrounds, abilities and dispositions
- demonstrate consistently the positive attitudes, values and behaviour which are expected of pupils

2. **Promote good progress and outcomes by pupils**
- be accountable for pupils' attainment, progress and outcomes
- plan teaching to build on pupils' capabilities and prior knowledge
- guide pupils to reflect on the progress they have made and their emerging needs
- demonstrate knowledge and understanding of how pupils learn and how this impacts on teaching
- encourage pupils to take a responsible and conscientious attitude to their own work and study

5. **Adapt teaching to respond to the strengths and needs of all pupils**
- have a clear understanding of the needs of all pupils, including those with special educational needs; those of high ability; those with English as an additional language; those with disabilities; and be able to use and evaluate distinctive teaching approaches to engage and support them

6. **Make accurate and productive use of assessment**
- know and understand how to assess the relevant subject and curriculum areas,

including statutory assessment requirements
- make use of formative and summative assessment to secure pupils' progress
- use relevant data to monitor progress, set targets, and plan subsequent lessons
- give pupils regular feedback, both orally and through accurate marking, and encourage pupils to respond to the feedback

Introduction

In the previous chapters, cross-curricular English teaching has been largely addressed without explicitly considering the details of differentiation and inclusion. In any classroom, teachers are required to address a range of diverse learning needs, including special educational needs, behavioural issues, gifted and talented pupils and those with pupils for whom English is an Additional Language (EAL). In recent years both the number and diversity of pupils speaking another language as a first language has increased. In 2011, the National Association for Language Development in the Curriculum reported that over a million school-aged children in the United Kingdom have English as an additional language. More than 360 different languages were recorded (NALDIC, 2011).

Many pupils from ethnic minority groups continue to underperform in school (Department for Education, 2008/2009). Limited capacities to speak, read and write English are often stated as a reason for this underachievement. This link is only partial, since some bilingual communities achieve to a far greater degree, such as some Asian pupils in comparison to some African-Caribbean pupils. Nevertheless, the presence of non English-speaking pupils in the classroom has presented trainees, teachers and managers with a number of challenges as well as providing opportunities to celebrate the richness associated with teaching and learning in a multicultural environment.

This chapter concentrates on practical ways to meet these challenges and to celebrate multiculturalism across the curriculum. It begins by describing the dual challenges of understanding a new language and the language of each curriculum subject. The chapter continues by discussing practical ways to address EAL pupils' access to the curriculum, curriculum planning for EAL pupils and applications of the key principles of teaching and learning for them. The chapter concludes with an example of cross-curricular planning for a class containing a number of EAL pupils.

Terminology

A number of technical terms appear in this chapter.

- **EAL** is an acronym for English as an Additional Language. It acknowledges the fact that some pupils already speak, and may also write, one or more languages.

- **Bilingual** refers to pupils who speak and hear further languages both at home and at school. The pupil may not be very fluent in any of the languages.

- **Cognitive, academic language proficiency (CALPS)** is a term coined by the influential EAL researcher Jim Cummins to describe a level of language acquisition that can take five to seven years to develop completely. It is the language necessary for academic and literacy proficiency (Hornberger and Baker, 2001).

- **Basic Interpersonal Communications Skills (BICS)** is a term coined by Cummins to describe a level of language acquisition that can take two to three years to develop completely. It is the language necessary for everyday, functional communication and conversation (Hornberger and Baker, 2001).

- **Minority ethnic group** describes the body of pupils other than the White British majority. In some schools with high levels of pupils with EAL minority ethnic groups may well be in the majority but nationally they are currently still members of a minority group.

- **Mono-cultural teaching** describes teaching that excludes the recognition of a multicultural society.

- **Meta-cognition** describes the pupils' knowledge of their own thought and the factors that influence their thinking. In EAL learners, meta-cognition benefits their ability to understand and separate the vocabulary of a subject from the language necessary to interpret it.

The need to differentiate for EAL learners across the curriculum

Pupils who speak English as an additional language have specific learning needs. This does not necessarily imply that a learning difficulty exists but instead that particular teaching approaches are necessary. It is important to make this distinction since EAL speakers, particularly in their early days of learning English, may be unable to access the curriculum and appear as if they possess learning difficulties. However, when considering how to meet the needs of EAL pupils, strands common to all types of inclusive and differentiated teaching are used. The Department for Education and Skills (DfES, 2002) produced a set of three teaching strands associated with addressing differentiation and inclusive teaching approaches for all pupils. These strands inform the structure of this chapter.

1. Access: the need to overcome potential barriers to learning and assessment for individuals and groups of pupils

2. Learning objectives: the need to set suitable learning challenges

3. Teaching styles: the need to respond to pupils' diverse needs

In addition to these general tenets, for pedagogical inclusivity and differentiation, there are a number of separate pedagogical approaches to meeting the needs of EAL pupils immersed into a mainstream school. In this chapter, an approach is used that unpacks the role of language across the curriculum. According to Cummins, it is necessary for EAL pupils to succeed in two types of language: cognitive and academic language proficiency (CALPS) and basic interpersonal communication skills (BICS) that is, language sufficient for functional and social interaction. The latter includes functional language necessary for actions like asking for the toilet and conversational speech. Cummins has indicated (Hornberger and Baker, 2001) that the full development of CALPS can take up to seven years, whereas BICS may take only two to three years to develop completely. Teachers, therefore, cannot afford to wait for a second language to develop naturally, or in a bilingual setting, nor can they realistically ask for sufficient English proficiency before the pupil enters school. Instead, teachers are required to facilitate EAL pupils to access the curriculum whilst promoting the individual development of English speech and comprehension. In order to do this, teachers must ensure that EAL pupils can both understand the necessary language and express the contents associated with each lesson taught in English. This means that they must recognise both the necessary concepts, vocabulary and sentence structures associated with the subject. It also includes those sentence structures that facilitate thinking and reasoning within each curriculum area.

Teachers have four primary responsibilities in addressing the needs of EAL learners.

1. To survey the range of languages spoken in the classroom and match it to the range of languages found in the school.
2. To assess and monitor the pupils' level of EAL acquisition.
3. To plan for EAL pupils in each lesson.
4. To incorporate appropriate school staff, parents and caregivers in the learning of EAL pupils.

All curriculum subjects present opportunities for class teachers to fulfil these responsibilities.

Enabling access to the curriculum

In this section, three key areas necessary for promoting access to cross-curricular learning in EAL learners are considered: language assessment, use of first languages and the recognition of multiple cultures and ethnicities.

In previous chapters, you were asked to consider the teaching of English from the perspective of curriculum content. You were asked to consider how particular reading, writing, speaking and listening activities might be employed to address the breadth of the primary National Curriculum. These activities may have surprised you in that you may not have considered the multiple layers of meaning evident in all these activities. This raises the question as to how pupils make those leaps from concrete to abstract comprehension and thinking skills necessary for such cross-curricular focused work. In EAL pupils the issues of how, when and why to make these links transparent to the pupil is an integral part of the process of acquiring English and accessing the whole curriculum. An accurate English language assessment is basic to this process.

Language assessment

Accurate assessment of pupils' level of English acquisition is fundamental to effective cross-curricular teaching of EAL pupils. While periods of language revision can supplement second language development, poorly pitched lessons can result in delayed or impaired language development for EAL pupils.

Language assessment need not always be formal. For example, each lesson that includes EAL pupils should begin by providing time and structures to recall and express what they know about the topic in question. Structures categorise vocabulary and concepts. Visual structures, or graphic organisers, such as Venn diagrams or KWL grids (what the pupil knows, wants to know and what has been learnt in that lesson) facilitate this process. Further details of these graphic organising tools occur in the non-fiction chapter of this book and in the final section of this chapter. In this way, teachers can make a formative assessment of what relevant vocabulary is already known.

The following table summarises stages of second language acquisition based on the principles of natural communication (Krashen and Terrell, 1983). Not every child will pass through every stage because each child will be at a different stage of second language acquisition. Other summaries of the stages of second language acquisition exist and can be sourced from bodies such as NALDIC.

1. Before speech	2. Early speech	3. Speech	4. Irregular fluency	5. Fluency
Listening and observing, more than speaking	Limited speech	Simple sentences and errors	Complex sentences and errors	Errors are self-corrected
Minimal comprehension	Narrow comprehension		Wider comprehension	Effective comprehension

Using first languages in the primary classroom

All children come to school with different levels of linguistic competence and a variety of different language experiences on which to build. Building on these meta-cognitive and cultural circumstances is particularly important for EAL pupils because it expands the contexts from which language can develop. This includes utilising the children's first language in the classroom where it is appropriate to do so.

Research Focus

North American research suggests that using the first language of pupils with EAL has a beneficial effect on learning English (Reese et al., 2000). In more recent case study research of British ethnic minority pupils, it was discovered that although schools followed National Curriculum guidelines and encouraged the use of home languages, wherever it was appropriate, the day-to-day reality was quite different (Pagett, 2006). These pupils were reluctant to use their home language in school. It was seen as neither productive nor necessary. In addition, the pupils did not want to appear different to the majority of their peers. In contrast, the pupils communicated in different languages at home. They code switched (used words from both languages at once) and used what Pagett has termed 'bilingual parallel speech'. Here the pupils responded in English to the parent speaking to them in their home language.

Recognising multiple cultures and ethnicities in the primary school

While pupils with EAL have a wide range of linguistic ability, it is also important to consider the pupils' language histories since this can provide a useful context for planning for EAL pupils across the curriculum, alongside their non-EAL peers. One of the easiest ways to collate this information is by conducting a whole class language survey. Ideally, this exercise should also be completed for the whole school population. Possible headings may include the following.

1. Full name
2. Age
3. Gender
4. Language spoken at home
5. Language written and read
6. Country of origin
7. Date started school in UK
8. Stage of acquiring English
9. Special educational need
10. Possible refugee status

Successful data collection like this enables simple classroom strategies to occur like grouping pupils according to common languages and language experiences. It is essential that the class teacher and the pupils approach activities like this with a positive attitude towards language diversity, particularly if mono-cultural teaching has figured in the past.

Activity

Information from surveys like this can also be used to encourage all pupils to be aware of variations in language within their own homes and communities. In order for you to become aware of your own language history, consider the following questions.

1. What is your first language?
2. How many other languages do you speak?
3. Apart from in your first language can you read a novel in another language?
4. Would you consider writing in another language as a regular occurrence?
5. Do you consider that you use a dialect?
6. Do you consider that you have an accent?

Once the diversity of EAL pupils in the class is identified, the use of culturally relevant material can enhance the language potential of their progress.

Case Study: Cross-cultural/cross-curriculum teaching

John is an NQT in his first term of class teaching. He is teaching in a mixed age group class of 30 Year 5 and Year 6 pupils, 40 per cent of whom have Polish as their first language. John is keen to establish positive working relationships with his new class as well as to set up the necessary rules for behaviour and work expectations that he hopes will be a characteristic of the ethos in his first classroom. Part of the religious education syllabus for that term specifies that pupils learn about religious faith as part of a local community. The geography and history topics for that term focus on the history and geography of the local community.

John uses the information from the language studies to plot where the pupils have come from in Poland and England on large maps of the UK and Poland. Using the Internet, he encourages groups of pupils to work with peers who speak the same first language. They draw up plans of the religious buildings and local amenities in the contrasting localities of Poland and the UK. To the pupils' surprise, there are many similarities as well as significant differences. Many Polish pupils come from Krakow. Each group prepares a small oral presentation for the class.

In the second half of the term, John pairs Polish speakers with native English speaking pupils and asks them to trace a significant historical figure in Krakow and the local philanthropist who endowed the local parks to their people of their local UK town.

Alongside this activity, John encourages pupils to write and draw their reading histories: a visual representation of the history of their literary practices, books and literature that were meaningful to them since early childhood. In this way, he

→

gathers valuable information about pupils' previous reading and literacy practices out of school plus their levels of independent recreational reading. He uses this information to plan the contents of his small class library, his class books for reading aloud at story time and his guided reading groups for that term.

The pupils liked discovering the similarities and differences between the members of their class. Overall, it provided a basis for a classroom ethos based on mutual respect for diversity and achievement.

Links to the National Curriculum

Children were developing their awareness of the similarities and differences among cultures, ethnicities, races and religion in personal, social and health education. They were also increasing their geographical understanding of the area in which they live as well as their historical understanding of the area in which they live. Furthermore, by understanding and appreciating literary texts, the children's reading motivation and personal reading repertoire was increased.

Learning objectives: the need to set suitable learning challenges

Language skills develop through the integration of the four modes of English.

- Listening: pupils understand speech
- Speaking: pupils can convey their thoughts through speech
- Reading: pupils can decode and comprehend text
- Writing: pupils can write words and phrases

These four modes underpin the entire primary curriculum. For all pupils, achievement from cross-curricular teaching is characterised by their ability to integrate and apply the four modes of English in language they can speak and understand. EAL learners have the additional challenges of applying their knowledge of the English language, and understanding the cultural and linguistic contexts of each curriculum subject and of making the necessary links between them.

Jim Cummins adds to this framework through his descriptions of how EAL learners best (Cummins, 2000; Hornberger and Baker, 2001). Cummins showed that effective teachers of EAL learners planned learning that showed both a relevant context and a suitable level of cognitive demand. In practice, this means providing opportunities for children to reflect and to experience multi-sensory activities that allow language practice. These ideas spring from psychological principles that advocate the development of language in social contexts, sometimes called social constructivism. The figure below represents an adapted version of

Cummins' ideas together with examples of classroom activities or approaches that may occur within each section. Initially, teachers need to aim for teaching approaches within quadrant B, while working towards achievement in quadrant A.

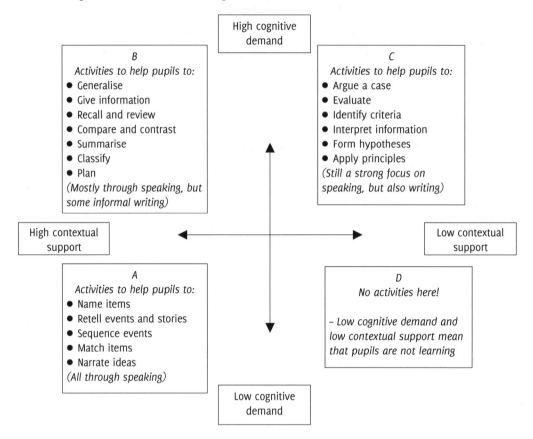

Figure 5.1 Preparing for Language differentiation for EAL learners (adapted from Cummins, 2001)

Activity
Multi-sensory teaching
Language itself is abstract but it is used to describe real things. Where possible, using real experiences brings language to life. This is important because pupils will remember what they can see and do.

Multi-sensory teaching for EAL learners is characterised by the use of visual cues, gesture, body language, diagrams, pictures, concrete examples and talk in both the home language and in English. Complete the table on page 87 to record what changes need to be made in order to accommodate the multi-sensory needs of EAL learners.

Subject	NC Ref	Activity	Year group	Multi-sensory adaptation
Geography	2a,c,d	Draw and label a walking map from home to school using primary and secondary sources of information	4	Teacher models use of maps around school and classroom. Use toy figures to 'walk' the routes to different destinations on a local map. Physically walk the route to school using a camera to record key landmarks. Use satellite images to match these photographs to them. Plot the route to school, with labelled photographs in sequential order on a route map
Drama (Speaking and Listening)	2a 6a,b,c,	Readers Theatre: Improvise sections of the class novel read in story time that includes questioning of the characters' motives	3	
Music	2b	Make an audio recording to represent a trip to the beach	2	
Art or Design and Technology	Art 2a D&T 1a-d 2a-e	Create a toy using a box or a classroom chair as a basic structure	6	

Reading and EAL learners

Teaching EAL children to read from scratch is beyond the remit of this book. Many EAL pupils, who have learned to read beyond a basic level in their first language, transfer some of their literacy knowledge to reading in the second. A number of key principles apply when selecting and using texts for EAL pupils to read in cross-curricular activities.

- Reading material should be within the children's own experience. If necessary support the children's understanding with a range of real experiences and objects related to the text.

- Reading many short whole texts (approximately 100 words) rather than sections of text, encourages understanding of grammatical structures and whole themes (this is called textual cohesion).

- Reading material should encourage prediction, especially if it is a new concept.

- Repetitive sentence structures and repeated readings of familiar texts encourages prediction.

- Aim to talk about the text before reading. This gives the pupil opportunities to hear unfamiliar words and phrases as well as to pick up the repetition of new ones.

- Aim to use picture clues to support understanding.

- Aim to use pupils' implicit knowledge of grammar from their first language; rereading the text can do this.

- Aim for a high capacity to both decode and recognise whole words automatically.

- Model the use of a range of strategies to decode text: sight vocabulary, word-shape cues, phonic cues, and picture cues, reading back and reading on. It is particularly important to demonstrate the different approaches to reading fiction and non-fiction texts, using open questions to encourage the pupils' interest in the text.

The following case study illustrates the integration of these key concepts in a cross-curricular music based project with a Year 3 class. Note how the trainee teacher has used other children and adults to provide opportunities for repetition and practice of key language in a number of different situations.

Case Study: Exploring the heritage of songs, stories, rhymes and poems

Winston is in his second placement. He has been placed in Year 3 of an inner city school where 50 per cent of the pupils have English as an additional language. The school has about fourteen different languages represented in its community. In his Year 3 class, a majority of the EAL pupils have good BICS language and can decode texts but more work is necessary to develop prediction and recall. Winston has been asked to plan the Year 3 unit on poetry that is to last two weeks. In college, he has been involved in weekly sharing of pupils' literature since the first days of his course. Recently the focus has been on poetry and multicultural texts, including dual language books with language play in them such as in tongue twisters and word games. In school, he plans a carefully sequenced set of activities based on the universal theme of food. The local library supplies a range of poetry books from around the world. He plans a sequence of activities that move from shared reading of repetitive poetry that also includes narrative, rhymes, songs and singing playground games. He recruits some parent volunteers to introduce repetitive songs and playground games to the class that are common in their respective cultures. The unit culminates in a performance of poetry and song from the pupils and the parents in school assembly. It includes role-play of the narrative poems. The pupils, class teachers and parents also produce home-made books of the poems and playground songs in a set of dual language texts that are added to the class library. Finally, mixed pairs of EAL and non-EAL pupils take these books to share with pupils in Key Stage 1.

This sequence of activities allows the EAL pupils to consolidate familiar concepts in the new context of songs, rhymes and poetry both in their home language and in English. It also provides a platform for the non-EAL pupils to access the heritage of their own playground songs and rhymes and narrative poetry.

Links to the National Curriculum

In the case study the children developed their performance and singing and aural memory in music and their reading and comprehension skills associated with poetry and song from a range of cultures in English. They also developed their ability to evaluate and develop ideas in art and design. The book-making work provided opportunities to adapt the text and illustrations for a KS1 audience.

Storytelling

The use of storytelling is a powerful tool for providing a context for EAL learning. Encouraging storytelling in different languages is a useful way into this process. Here parents, support assistants and specialist EAL teachers can be an invaluable resource. The key principles of reading with EAL learners also apply to storytelling. Texts must have accompanying pictures, repetitive texts and be within the pupils' experience. Storytelling provides opportunities to rehearse and consolidate the language associated with particular cross-curricular subjects. It can include oral storytelling and story making around culturally relevant activities. For example, using ICT to make digital stories is especially useful to EAL because it incorporates diverse opportunities for language rich interaction with English and native speakers.

Research Focus

As pupils progress into Key Stage 2, more information is gained from the printed word as well as from spoken language. Key Stage 3 research from North America is also relevant to primary teachers (Ivey and Broaddhus, 2007). This intervention study highlights the necessity of providing specific types of texts to motivate and engage EAL pupils in personal and academic reading. Broadly, these texts are culturally relevant, self-selected reading materials that integrate the process of reading and writing. Four types of text have particular value.

1. Word-less picture books: when used alongside related dictations these texts provided a bridge with writing instruction. Meaning is confirmed using the picture, gesture or by confirming with a bilingual dictionary.
2. Emergent concept books that provide limited texts with real life pictures, counting books are an example. The repetitive nature of these books supports independent reading.
3. Picture books that highlight spoken language; these are often simple strip cartoons with speech bubbles. These work well for teachers to read aloud, where expression and idiomatic speech can be demonstrated and explained. They are useful texts to promote role-play and the production of storyboards.
4. Menus, signs, letters, directions and other examples of instructional language provide experience of reading in different formats and provide a bridge to writing in different genres.

Writing and EAL learners

A number of key principles apply when developing writing for EAL pupils to write in cross-curricular activities.

- Aim to develop clause and sentence level grammar: adverbial phrases, the breadth of descriptive noun and verb phrases, the use of tenses, pronouns, determiners, prepositions and short phrases (Cameron and Bessener, 2004).

- Aim to develop subject specific vocabulary.

- Aim to create a print rich classroom environment. Label key fixtures and fittings. Provide a visual daily timetable with English captions. Provide word walls of key subject vocabulary and wall mounted pouches of key words in alphabetical order. Tabletop versions add to this resource.

- Encourage pupils to write in their own language on some occasions. Making personal bilingual books is an example.

- Provide themes that enable pupils to write from personal experience.

- Aim to develop knowledge of text types or genres. Model the structures of different genres preceded by immersing pupils in reading many examples of them.

- Use personalised writing frames. They may contain picture cues or fragments of the first language, for instance.

- Aim to promote shared writing. Plan writing that is preceded by active role-play, or real life experiences and finally by plenty of discussion.

Activity

Look at this example of Year 6 writing from a history topic on ancient civilisations. The pupil with EAL was retelling a myth he had previously studied. How many of the EAL writing issues highlighted above can you identify? Are there any additional matters to address? What practical strategies from the list above would assist you in addressing this pupil's writing needs?

> King Ariculos lived in Argos and he have a son called Dane. 'She will have a son called Perseus and he will killed him. The king out them in chest and push them the shore of Sepharios. Dydycus found them. Dydcus bring them to the king called King Polydectus. King Polydectus fell in love with Dane but he propose every opportunity. The king told Perseus to get the head of Medusa to kill the king so Perseus travelled far far away but he can' t see as sight of Medusa and some warrior women came and give him a sord sickle.
>
> He nicked the eye and one toot they have a deal for inforaiont so they tell Perseus and he got that cave and he found the uglyest monster called Medusa

> The Hermes told Perseus to go to the three aglee sisters the Hermies say to got to the gray ones the Perseus went to the cave.
>
> He fight Medusa but Perseus look at the shield, Perseus didn't, become stone. Perseus cut Medusas head off put Medusa head to his bag. In a minute Medusas sister's woke up the Persus wore the helmet and the sun was giving the helmet more power suddenly Medusas sisters can't find the mysterious people who killed there sister there are shaking to anger because there sister medus the loveliest was killed.
>
> Percius back at the serapous but its not easy to go back after he saw his mother hiding to the king and the king saw Perseus alive. Perserus take incredible head of medusa the king became to stone and they squashed medusas head after that. They crowned king Dycties to be the new king. Percius and his mother set off in Argos and they leave happily ever after.

You may have noted additional needs for discrete grammar teaching. Tense and pronouns need some attention as do sentence structures. Practical activities to address this including manipulating the parts of a sentence with pre-prepared sentences, written on coloured cards. Such activities require pupils with EAL to rehearse English by speaking it before writing.

Addressing needs like this requires focussed teaching in guided writing both within and outside of the English lesson coupled with accurate assessment. Writing development in EAL pupils also thrives when taught in a cross-curricular manner that integrates the four modes of English: reading, writing, speaking and listening.

Case Study: Nature walks and Concept Cartoons in science

Jo is a PGCE pupil approaching her final placement. She has been placed in a Year 2 class, 20 per cent of whom speak Nepalese as a first language. The majority of the Nepalese pupils are new arrivals. Jo suspects that at least five pupils are still in the 'silent period' of absorbing English. In science, the pupils have been looking at how green plants grow. Jo is keen to encourage group discussion and real life experiences. She begins the unit by taking the class on a nature walk in the school's 'wild area' of natural space attached to the school grounds. The pupils are specifically grouped in threes, one EAL pupil with two competent speakers of English. Each group of pupils is directed to a specific part of the 'wild area' to either draw or photograph three of the plants growing there. In the classroom, the photographs and drawings are collated to make a visual class map of the 'wild area'. The different areas and common plants are labelled and described by the pupils. The support assistant provides amanuensis for the EAL pupils at this stage. Alongside these activities, the pupils grow cress seeds in halves of an eggshell. In

→

mixed ability groups of three, the pupils use a Concept Cartoon (Naylor and Keogh, 2002) to discuss the effect of light on the cress seeds. They place some seeds in the dark and some in the light to test their predictions. Discussions are recorded on simple writing frames previously modelled and adapted by the class teacher. When the wild area maps and cress eggshells were compared to those of a parallel class, the pupils were able to see the similarities and differences between them and began to use phrases to describe what they saw as part of their small group. This unit of work concentrates on the elaboration of concepts, rather than simplification of them. They also provide opportunities for pupils to ask questions and to gather data in real life situations.

Links to the National Curriculum

Undertaking this cross-curricular work enabled the children to develop scientific knowledge of the basic parts of a green plant and where plants grow in the immediate environment. They also developed geographical enquiry skills and knowledge and understanding of different places.

Teaching styles: the need to respond to pupils' diverse needs

In this section, three key areas necessary for responding to the diverse needs of EAL learners across the curriculum are considered: scaffolding, modelling and questioning. Modelling is demonstration. Modelling allows the pupil to see what is required. Scaffolding is the process of setting up structures that enable the pupil to build on relevant language and conceptual knowledge. Questioning can be a form of assessment and of scaffolding. Closed, rhetorical or open questions allow the pupil to recall and rehearse understanding in a range of different contexts. Responding to the diverse needs of EAL learners also means utilising a range of other adults to support them.

The following table presents a weekly English plan produced as part of a cross-curricular week on the theme of rainforests. The Year 4 class has 10 per cent of its members from Somalia.

Activity

Note how the plan accommodates the needs of the EAL learners, the number of other curriculum subjects that link to the plan and the use of other adults. Note the opportunities for modelling, questioning and scaffolding in whole class, group and individual situations.

Learning objectives: Understand principles of rainforest destruction			Learning outcomes: Present digital story of Jennie Baker's 'Where the Forest Meets the Sea'		
Session	NC link	Shared learning and teaching	Independent learning	Assessment criteria	Guided learning
1	English KS2 En1 3a-e En2 9b Geography: KS2 1d 1e	Relate to own experiences. Show newsreel clip of road building destroying local area of natural beauty	Use differentiated writing frames to record local story. EAL groups with support assistant to match and extend captions to screen shots	Use thinking cubes with each ability group in plenary. Thinking cubes based on Bloom's taxonomy (Bloom, 1956)	Group C: able non-EAL readers discuss newspaper article attached to newsreel clip. Make audio recording of mock interviews with protagonists
2	Geography: KS2 2c	Share read: 'Where the Forest Meets the Sea' (Baker, 1987). Use world map to locate rainforest in story	Place pupils in mixed ability groups. What are the similarities between the story and their experiences?	Record on Venn diagram	Group A: mixed ability plus EAL stage 1 acquisition. Discuss rainforest language in book and develop labels for copies of key pages of Baker story. Build key words charts
3	Geography: KS2 1d 1e 2g English: KS2 En1 2a 2b 2c En2 9b	Revise Baker's book by looking at the animated version of the book Hot seating of main protagonists in story	Place the pupils in mixed ability pairs to record on Y charts sounds, sights and feelings as you watch the film	Record on Y chart	Group B: mixed ability plus EAL stage 2 acquisition. Develop speech bubbles to match photographs of main protagonists in Baker story
4	ICT KS2: 2a 3b 1b Art: KS2 5a 5b 5c Maths: KS2 Ma3, 4b 4e 1 Ma4 1f, 1g 1h English KS2 En1 3a-e	Use story plan to rewrite Baker story in shared writing Keep bound version of shared story for class library	Three groups Prepare figures, scenes and props for digital story	Write a list of characters, scenes or props for the digital story. Present under sketches as captions	SEN readers: read and discuss familiar themes in comparative rainforest storybook
5	ICT KS2: 2a 3b 1b Art KS2 5a 5b 5c Maths KS2 Ma3, 4b 4e 1 Ma4 1f, 1g ,1h English KS2 En1 3a-e	Complete shared writing of story Leads to performance at parent's afternoon at end of cross-curricular week	Complete props, scenes and figures necessary for digital story Use ICT film-making package to shoot film using class shared story as narrative	Use thinking cubes with each ability group in plenary. Thinking cubes based on Bloom's taxonomy	Middle readers: discuss familiar themes in comparative rainforest storybook

Table 6.1 Cross-curricular weekly English plan for Year 4: Rainforests

Learning Outcomes Review

This chapter has explored the needs of EAL learners. It has given a broad range of examples of cross-curricular teaching founded in key principles that facilitate EAL learning. Throughout your classroom career, you will be required to address issues of differentiation and inclusion in all aspects of school life. Establishing key techniques and principles in cross-curricular teaching will enable EAL children to feel valued and challenged in their learning while at school.

Self-assessment questions

1. Provide at least three reasons for using other adults to assist with EAL learning.
2. List the key features of a classroom environment for EAL learners in KS1 and KS2.
3. List ten top tips for effectively meeting the needs of EAL pupils with a range of other languages who are in one classroom.

Further Reading and Resources

www.naldic.org.uk
This organisation provides resources and research for EAL pupils.

www.mantralingua.com
This organisation sources dual language books and resources.

Excellence and Enjoyment: Learning and teaching bilingual students in the primary years (DfES 0013-20006DCL-EN).
The resource provides materials for addressing EAL across the curriculum.

Conteh, J. (2012) *Teaching Bilingual and EAL Learners in Primary Schools*. London: Learning Matters.
This book encourages you to carefully consider the children who come under the umbrella of EAL and provides practical strategies for inclusive teaching.

Thinking cubes available from www.LDAlearning.com

References

Baker, J. (1987) *Where the Forest Meets the Sea*. London: Walker Books.

Bloom B.S. (1956) *Taxonomy of Educational Objectives, Handbook I: The Cognitive Domain*. New York: David McKay Co Inc.

Cameron, L. and Bessener, S. (2004) *Writing in English as an additional language at KS2: DfES research report 586*. London.

Cummins, J. (2000) *Language, power and pedagogy: Bilingual children in the crossfire.* Clevedon: Multilingual Matters.

Cummins, J. (2001) *Negotiating Identities: Education for employment in a diverse society* (2nd edition). Los Angeles: California Association for Bilingual Education.

Department for Education (2008/2009) Key Stage 2 Attainment by Pupil Characteristics, in England. Publication. Retrieved October 2011, from Department for Education: http://www.dcsf.gov.uk/rsgateway/DB/SFR/s000889/index.shtml

Department for Education and Skills (2002) *Supporting pupils learning English as an additional language.* London: DfES.

Department for Education and Skills (2003) *Aiming High: Raising the achievement of minority ethnic pupils.* London: DfES.

Hornberger, N.H. and Baker, C. (eds) (2001) *An introductory reader to the writings of Jim Cummins.* Clevedon: Multilingual Matters.

Ivey, G. and Broaddus, K. (2007) A formative experiment investigating literacy engagement among Latino adolescents just beginning to read, write and speak English. *Reading Research Quarterly*, 42(4), 512–545.

Krashen, S.D. and Terrell, T.D. (1983) *The natural approach: Language acquisition in the classroom.* London: Prentice Hall.

NALDIC (2011) EAL Statistics. The latest EAL facts and figures. Retrieved 12.3.2012 from www.naldic.org.uk/research-and-information/eal-statistics

Naylor, S. and Keogh, B. (2002) *Concept Cartoons in Science Education.* Crewe, Cheshire, UK: Millgate House Publishers.

Pagett, L. (2006) Mum and Dad prefer me to speak Bengali at home: Code switching and parallel speech in a primary school setting. *Literacy*, 40(3), 137–145.

Reese, I., Garnier, H., Gallimore, R. and Goldenberg, C. (2000) Longitudinal analysis of the antecedents of emergent Spanish literacy and middle school English reading achievement of Spanish-speaking students. *American Educational Research Journal*, 37(3), 622–633.

6. Thinking skills

Learning Outcomes

This chapter aims to help you to:

- develop your understanding about what is meant by 'thinking skills';
- consider why these skills should be taught to support English and cross-curricular learning;
- be introduced to the skills that children need to develop so that they become good thinkers in English and cross-curricular learning;
- become aware of the strategies and resources available to support children in developing good thinking skills.

TEACHERS' STANDARDS

A teacher must:

1. Set high expectations which inspire, motivate and challenge pupils

- establish a safe and stimulating environment for pupils, rooted in mutual respect
- set goals that stretch and challenge pupils of all backgrounds, abilities and dispositions
- demonstrate consistently the positive attitudes, values and behaviour which are expected of pupils

2. Promote good progress and outcomes by pupils

- be accountable for pupils' attainment, progress and outcomes
- plan teaching to build on pupils' capabilities and prior knowledge
- guide pupils to reflect on the progress they have made and their emerging needs
- demonstrate knowledge and understanding of how pupils learn and how this impacts on teaching
- encourage pupils to take a responsible and conscientious attitude to their own work and study

3. Demonstrate good subject and curriculum knowledge

- have a secure knowledge of the relevant subject(s) and curriculum areas, foster and maintain pupils' interest in the subject, and address misunderstandings
- demonstrate a critical understanding of developments in the subject and curriculum areas, and promote the value of scholarship
- demonstrate an understanding of and take responsibility for promoting high standards of literacy, articulacy and the correct use of standard English, whatever the teacher's specialist subject

4. **Plan and teach well structured lessons**
- impart knowledge and develop understanding through effective use of lesson time
- promote a love of learning and children's intellectual curiosity
- reflect systematically on the effectiveness of lessons and approaches to teaching
- contribute to the design and provision of an engaging curriculum within the relevant subject area(s)

5. **Adapt teaching to respond to the strengths and needs of all pupils**
- know when and how to differentiate appropriately, using approaches which enable pupils to be taught effectively

Introduction

This chapter considers what is meant by the term *thinking skills* and asks you to reflect upon what you already know about these skills. Why these skills are relevant to teaching English and other curriculum subjects in schools today is explored. Recent theory and research which has influenced the teaching of thinking skills is considered in an historical context. What constitutes good thinking and the different kinds of thinking that you should be encouraging in your classrooms is discussed. Finally we explore the variety of strategies and resources available to help you in supporting children to develop these skills.

What is meant by the term thinking skills?

In most schools thinking skills do not appear as a separate subject on the timetable but most children spend a great deal of time involved in related activity. You will probably have heard teachers asking children 'to think about...' a point raised during a lesson and then an opportunity will be given for children to discuss and share the results of their thinking. You need to consider what is happening and what you intend to happen when you ask children to think and discuss the results of their thinking.

Activity
Thinking about thinking skills
As you start this chapter answer the following questions.

- What do you understand is meant by the term thinking skills?
- Do you believe that these skills can be taught?
- What is a good thinker?
- Are thinking skills a valuable part of a child's education?
- Have you observed any thinking skills activities?

As you read this chapter add to your ideas and thoughts on this subject.

A Year 6 child was overheard to state after an English lesson: 'My brain hurts because I have been working hard'. The girl had not completed any writing during the session but had been involved in thinking and talking about the motives for the actions of one of the characters in the book the group were reading. The child recognised that thinking was an active process and required a great deal of effort on the part of the thinker. So what was happening to challenge this child during this lesson?

Adey et al. (2001) describe the thinking process as:

> Something we do when we try to solve problems; it involves processing the information that we have available to us – either from the external world or from within our own memories. Thinking allows us to take things we know or observe and turn them into new ways of understanding'.

> (Adey et al., 2001, page 2)

This statement by Adey et al. makes clear that the aim of the thinking process is to solve problems and develop new ways of understanding but what is the 'something we do' to achieve these aims? It is a complex process and still not completely understood but there is agreement among researchers (Alexander, 2008; Lipman, 2003) about some of the processes and skills involved in successful thinking.

First, and most importantly, earlier chapters identified the central role language plays in supporting children to develop as successful and effective thinkers. Language is the tool of thinking and it is required by children for both their *inner thinking voice*, a concept first identified by Vygotsky (1986) and their *social voice* and opportunities are required for both kinds of voices to develop. Secondly, it has been observed that much productive thinking takes place in a social context. The social aspects of thinking provide opportunities for children to develop and practise thinking skills in pairs, groups and class situations. Finally it has been established that to be successful in developing a range of thinking skills children need to apply clearly structured rules of logic. To develop their knowledge and understanding of these rules it is essential that children are provided with opportunities and support. These three are all essential components of the thinking process and we explore and discuss strategies and resources for you to support children later in the chapter but it is relevant to consider briefly where our ideas on thinking skills have originated and how they influence our ideas on teaching today.

Research Focus

Our knowledge about thinking has developed from two main disciplines, first from the Greek philosophers such as Socrates and later from Plato and Aristotle. They believed in the importance of logic and dialogue which encouraged students to

→

develop new ideas and test them critically. Second, during the early twentieth century, ideas about thinking were developed by psychologists. Two influential educational psychologists were Piaget and Vygotsky. Piaget believed that children's thinking developed in clearly defined stages and was the result of interaction with the world around them. In the 1970s researchers such as Donaldson (1978) challenged some of Piaget's ideas and the work of Vygotsky is now more influential. Vygotsky believed that thought and language could not exist without each other therefore language was essential for the development of thinking. He observed that articulating thoughts was necessary if children were to become logical and critical thinkers. He also believed that learning and thinking were social in their origins and that children required a social environment to develop these skills successfully. You can read more about these theories in Mooney (2000).

Why teach thinking skills?

Fisher (2005) states that for children to succeed in school and prepare for their future lives it is essential to teach thinking skills. He claims that teaching thinking enables children to develop new knowledge and understanding which supports them in being able to make decisions, solve problems and create new ideas.

Smith (2010) gives five main reasons for teaching thinking skills which are summarised below.

- Talking and thinking underpin most of the learning which takes place in school.
- Teaching these skills will help children reach their potential as learners.
- It will help children to lead happier and more fulfilled lives.
- Teaching these skills is likely to make what happens in the classroom more enjoyable.
- They are part of the National Curriculum.

(Smith, 2010, pages 8–13)

Research Focus

The National Curriculum (DfEE, 1999, page 22) embedded six key skills to help learners to improve their learning and performance in education, work and life. One of these key areas was thinking skills. The National Curriculum stated that by using thinking skills children can focus on knowing how to learn as well as knowing what to learn. The following key skills were embedded into the 2000 National Curriculum.

- Information-processing: This enables pupils to locate and collect relevant information, to sort, classify, sequence, compare and contrast, and to analyse part/whole relationships.

$\rightarrow$

- Reasoning skills: These enable pupils to give reasons for opinions and actions, to draw inferences and make deductions, to use precise language to explain what they think, and to make judgements and decisions informed by reasons or evidence.

- Enquiry skills: These enable pupils to ask relevant questions and define problems, to plan what to do and how to research, to predict outcomes and anticipate consequences, and to test conclusions and improve ideas.

- Creative thinking skills: These enable pupils to generate and extend ideas, to suggest hypotheses, to apply imagination, and to look for alternative innovative outcomes.

- Evaluative skills: These enable pupils to evaluate information, to judge the value of what they read, hear and do, to develop criteria for judging the value of their own and others' work or ideas, to have confidence in their judgements.

The importance of thinking skills continues to be highlighted. In the report shaping the framework of the 2014 National Curriculum, the Expert Panel (DfE, 2011, page 21) recommended that schools develop beyond the slimmed down statutory requirements of the new curriculum a 'local curriculum'. This allows schools to innovate and develop particular curricular interests such as integrating thinking skills across the school curriculum.

What kind of thinking do we want in the classroom?

We need to establish what skills are needed for children to become good thinkers before we can plan and develop strategies that support these skills. Broadly the aim should be to help children structure their thinking. This will include aiding the child to retrieve information, add new information, develop and evaluate their own ideas, make connections between relevant ideas and work successfully in a social context. It becomes more essential to provide a clear framework for structuring these skills as Bruner (1966) makes clear that it is important to focus on the *process* of thinking and learning rather than the end *product*.

It has been briefly stated that for children to develop effective thinking skills they need opportunities to work both independently and in a social situation. Alexander (2008) has been influential in establishing that good thinking skills rely on providing opportunities *for high-quality talk* within the classroom. He believes that talk is the foundation of learning and that linking talking and thinking is essential if children are to become effective learners.

As good thinking is so closely connected with talking, it is important to establish what constitutes the kind of talk you should encourage in your classroom. Alexander (2008, page 28) uses the term '*dialogic talk*' to describe five essential characteristics for supporting children develop successful talk. He states that classroom talk should be: collective, reciprocal, supportive, cumulative and purposeful. Fisher (2005) adds to this list of social skills for establishing good thinking skills the importance of supporting children to develop effective inner speech, which he defines as the ability of the child to talk to themselves.

This is an appropriate point to focus on different kinds of thinking skills and their relevance to English and cross-curricular learning. This is an area for discussion but Lipman (2003) has identified three main types of thinking; critical, creative and caring or collaborative thinking. Added to this is meta-cognition which are the set of skills needed to think about thinking. It is important for you to understand the different types of thinking children need if you are going to provide opportunities for children to acquire and practise these skills.

Critical thinking

Firstly critical thinking is also classified as convergent thinking. This is the processes by which children gather information, data or ideas and then use or analyse them for a clear purpose.

Creative thinking

Next creative thinking which is also classified as divergent or lateral thinking. Lipman (2003) identifies this kind of thinking as children's ability to see things in a new way. He believes that providing opportunities and encouraging children to explore a fresh view will encourage them to develop their own solutions to a problem or situation.

Caring or collaborative thinking

Lipman (2003) identifies the third skill, which he calls caring or collaborative thinking. He defines this thinking as the child's ability to co-operate with others in a social environment. He calls this social environment a *community* and he believes this community needs a clearly defined ethos which builds on respect for others, self esteem and empathy.

Meta-cognitive thinking

The fourth kind of thinking is *Meta-cognition* which Smith (2010, p 82) defines as *'the human ability to reflect upon experience and learn from it.'* Research by Hattie (2008) has clearly established that this is an essential skill for children to acquire if they are to be successful in school. This skill is vital to all areas of the curriculum as it supports children in becoming more independent learners so that they can organise and plan their learning and, importantly, make connections between different ideas and experiences.

Essential skills for good thinkers

By looking at the four types of thinking you have been introduced to some of the skills necessary for children to become good thinkers but it is important for you to consider this in more detail. Many researchers, including Ennis (2001), have attempted to do this. The main points agreed are that children need the skills to be able to:

- plan and structure their activities and work;
- gather information from a range of sources;
- be aware of the source of the information and take into account any bias;
- evaluate and interpret the information;
- recognise a problem;
- reflect on the situation;
- make connections between previous experience and new knowledge;
- draw conclusions and solve the problem;
- test the conclusion.

Underpinning this list is the skill children require to work successfully both independently and within a social group. It is therefore essential for you to consider and plan for this within your classroom.

What is your role?

Now we come to the crucial question: What can you do within the classroom to encourage and support children in developing good thinking skills? It is a challenge that has been the focus of educational enquiry and thought over the centuries. Over one hundred years ago Dewey (1910, page 13) made the claim that 'good thinking' is always:

> ... more or less troublesome because it involves overcoming the inertia that inclines one to accept suggestions at their face value; it involves willingness to endure a condition of mental unrest and disturbance... To maintain the state of doubt and to carry on systematic and protracted inquiry – these are the essentials of thinking.

The same challenges exist for you in the classroom today since good thinking is often not a comfortable process as it requires effort and determination on the part of the child. It also requires you to have knowledge about the strategies that are available to support you to teach these skills and Adey et al. (2001) and Fisher (2005) both emphasise the importance of your role in creating an appropriate environment.

It has already been stated that thinking should be an active, social and visible process and so it is important that you provide a classroom that encourages children to feel secure in expressing their own views and encourages them to be confident speakers and good listeners. This should include providing clear structures and frameworks within the classroom for which all children feel a responsibility and involvement to support and maintain. This might involve discussing class rules for organising speaking and listening activities or planning together how resources are shared and responsibilities distributed.

It is also important that you allow sufficient time for children to discuss and develop their ideas. Research by Taggart et al. (2005) has established that when children are allocated sustained thinking time they are more confident and able to reflect on their activities, review their work, develop further ideas and resolve challenge. The plenary of a lesson provides opportunities for you to develop this range of thinking and also allows you to encourage children to make connections between what has been learnt in this situation and how the information can be applied to other situations.

> ## Activity
> In your observations in school have you observed any activities that support children in developing their speaking and listening skills?
> Can you add to this list additional class activities that you think will support children in developing their confidence in becoming active speakers and listeners?

To support children in this social thinking process in the classroom it is essential that you provide opportunities for the children to acquire and use language for thinking and talking about thinking. This is called meta-cognition and has already been discussed. It is also important to remember that children acquire the linguistic skills to develop their thinking through the four modes of language, speaking and listening, reading and writing and these skills all need opportunities for the child to practise and develop.

Supporting children to develop good thinking skills in English and across the curriculum offers you opportunities to explore a range of strategies; it will often involve children working in a new and challenging way. It takes time and requires confidence on your part because a child will claim they are thinking when there is no evidence to support this statement: there is often no writing on the page, no diagram to be seen and no design under construction. It is therefore essential that you feel confident that the time you have devoted to developing these skills is well structured and organised.

Strategies for developing effective thinking skills

Fisher (2005) claims that all lessons should be lessons in thinking and therefore the strategies and resources available can be used across the curriculum. Some schools have established a whole school policy to implement and support children in developing the skills to become successful thinkers. Strategies such as the *Six Thinking Hats* (de Bono 2009) and *Community of Enquiry* (Lipman 2003) are used in many classrooms and as a whole school strategy. This part of the chapter will discuss some of the successful strategies being used in schools at present.

Parallel thinking

First we will discuss de Bono's ideas as he has been very influential in developing the teaching of thinking skills in school. His focus is on establishing techniques for what he calls *parallel* thinking in social groups and he gives the example of four people each standing on different sides of a building and each arguing that their side is the most beautiful. With de Bono's system of parallel thinking the four would each gather on one side of the building in turn and discuss the merits of each in sequence. He claims that the traditions of focusing on the adversarial aspects of thinking, such as arguing your case to win, were not helpful or constructive in encouraging thinking so he emphasises the importance of encouraging children to respect the opinions of others and give reasons why they agree or disagree.

De Bono has developed several strategies for developing parallel or lateral thinking which have been used successfully in schools throughout the world. We are going to look at one of his main strategies in more detail.

Cognitive research trust

De Bono has developed a range of techniques or what he calls *tools* which are part of the Cognitive research trust (CoRT) thinking programme that encourages lateral thinking. He calls them *attention-directing tools* and the aim behind the programme is to encourage children to focus on aspects of a situation that might not otherwise be considered. The programme also supports the teacher in providing a structure for the children's thinking. Two of his most tried and tested techniques are:

Plus, minus, interesting (PMI)

Children are asked to focus on three kinds of thinking in turn.

- plus – the good things about an idea. Why do you like it?
- minus – the bad things. Why don't you like it?
- interesting – what you find interesting about an idea and new ways of looking at it.

Case Study: Using the PMI strategy in a PSHE lesson

This case study illustrates how a trainee student used the PMI strategy to support children in his class to structure their thinking in a PSHE lesson.

Brian is on his final school experience and has been placed in a Year 3 class in a junior school. The children have recently moved from a separate infant school and the class teacher is concerned that some children in the class are finding it difficult to settle into the new environment. She discusses her concerns with Brian and they decide to use the PSHE lessons for developing strategies to support the children.

Brian had seen the PMI tool used in his previous school and suggests that this would be an appropriate strategy to encourage children to raise their concerns. The children were provided with a journal to record their thoughts. Brian began by asking the children to work with a partner and think/pair/share their ideas on what they most enjoyed about the new school and class. The think/pair/share strategy gives children the time and opportunity to reflect and develop their ideas before talking to a partner and eventually sharing their idea with the class. The children's comments were then shared and recorded in their journal.

$\rightarrow$

The following week Brian asked the children to record the things that concerned and worried them and in many cases he was able to develop strategies to overcome their concerns. Some concerns were shared by many children in the class for example the introduction of homework. Brian then introduced the *interesting* section of the PMI model and after discussion with the class teacher it was agreed that the children should be given longer to complete their homework task.

One child in the class was able to express her concern that her mother was no longer able to collect her from the classroom at the end of the school day and she was worried about finding her. Brian was able to accompany the child into the playground until she had gained enough confidence to do this on her own. The children continued to use their books to record their feelings using the *plus, minus and interesting model*. Brian and the class teacher were able to monitor and observe the children and discuss the concerns as they arose. Some of the issues were discussed during circle time and the children were often able to find a solution to solve their concerns. Brian and the class teacher both felt that by using this method the children were more confident in expressing and recording their concerns and were able to support each other in suggesting solutions to the situation.

Links to the National Curriculum

Many links to PSHE are evident in this activity as it supports children in reflecting on their own experiences across and beyond the curriculum. They are developing confidence and recognising what they like and dislike and also considering what is fair and unfair. They are developing the skills to share their feelings with others and to explain their views and deal with their feelings in a positive way. They are also developing the ability to play an active role as citizens by taking part in discussions with one other person and the whole class and to understand and agree to follow rules for their group.

In English the children are developing the ability to listen, understand and respond appropriately to other pupils and to make relevant contributions. They are developing their composition skills to suit a particular purpose and exploring their feelings, ideas and developing their thinking to solve problems.

The second strategy developed by De Bono is called the six thinking hats and it also supports children in developing structured ways of thinking. The technique uses six differently coloured hats. Each hat has a distinct role and the children are metaphorically encouraged to think in the style of each hat focusing on one kind of thinking at a time. For example the white hat has a focus on collecting information while the green hat encourages children to discuss new ideas and modify existing ones. More information about this method of thinking can be found in De Bono (2009) or edwdebono@msn.com

Philosophy for children

Philosophy for children (P4C) and the ideas behind this strategy were developed by Lipman to support the teaching of higher order thinking skills. One of the main structures used in schools to support this philosophy is the community of enquiry (spelt inquiry by Lipman). Lipman (2003) defined the community as a method of learning together and the structure encouraged the children to focus on the issues that they considered important.

The class work together to reflect and develop their thinking skills as a group with a shared structure and ethos. Children set their own questions and vote on which one they wish to discuss. The teacher acts as a facilitator and does not influence the selection of the question as this encourages the motivation of pupils and their involvement in the task. The questions raised by the children are discussed within a framework of three different types of thinking which Lipman identified as critical, creative and caring. The discussion takes place within a clear framework which is understood and adhered to by all children taking part in the discussion. This will include taking turns to talk, listening skills, giving reasons for statements and being respectful to others' opinions. It will also include encouraging the children to be brave talkers so that all the class feel capable and confident enough to contribute to the discussion. The child who selects the chosen question is given the opportunity to begin the discussion and can nominate the child chosen to speak next.

Case Study: Using the structure of the community of enquiry for a cross-curricular topic

Marie, who is on her final placement on a PGCE course, was appointed to a Year 2 class. The children in her class are used to working within the structure of the community of enquiry and are familiar with the rules. Marie was asked to plan a cross-curricular project with a focus on the environment. She selected the book 'Dinosaurs and All that Rubbish' by Michael Forman which introduces an environmental theme in a fiction text. The story introduces a man who in his desire to explore another planet leaves his own planet a barren waste. Marie read the book to the children in a literacy lesson and then asked the children to select a question they wished to discuss. They discussed their question with a partner and then the questions were recorded by Marie on the interactive whiteboard. The children therefore had an opportunity to see all the questions and were asked to vote for the question they wished to discuss as this encourages them to have a sense of involvement and ownership in the activity. The question the children selected was 'Why did the man want to go to the star?' The child who asked this question started the discussion using the structures of the community which provided opportunities for all children to contribute if they wanted to do so.

→

Children were encouraged to be brave talkers and give reasons for their opinions. Marie and the teacher were able to monitor the discussion which raised other questions such as: Why was the man destroying the planet? Will the man and the dinosaurs be able to live together and look after the planet? These questions were used by Marie and the class teacher to plan the next session which focused on how resources on the planet can be sustained and the environment be improved.

Links to the National Curriculum

Links to the English curriculum include providing opportunities for the children to develop their speaking skills by organising what they say, focusing on the main points and taking into account the needs of their listeners. In a group situation children take turns to speak, extend their ideas in the light of other children's contributions and give reasons for their opinions and actions. The topic develops links to geography by extending their knowledge and understanding of places which includes describing what places are like, recognising how places have become the way they are and how they are changing. It also provides opportunities for children to develop their knowledge and understanding of environmental changes and sustainable development.

Thinking actively in a social context

This method of supporting children to develop logical and reflective thinking skills also focuses on the importance of a social context and is known as TASC. This approach was devised by Wallace (2002) and establishes a framework for children to tackle problems in a systematic way. The method shares many of the same ideas as P4C but uses the structure of a TASC wheel.

Copyright © Belle Wallace 2000

Figure 6.1 The TASC Wheel

As can be seen the wheel has eight segments which are summed up in the phrase *Plan, Do and Review*. The children begin in the top right segment which has the heading gather/organise but the steps do not have to be followed rigidly as the TASC wheel can be adapted to suit the task you have planned. Each segment of the wheel has a suggested question which can start the thinking process and help in identifying the focus for that section of the wheel.

Statement games

A group of children are asked to arrange statements in order of importance. The statements are arranged in either a triangle or diamond and the statement that is considered the most important is placed at the top. Statements can either be provided for the children or the children can be encouraged to contribute their own statements. This is an appropriate activity for children to tackle at the end of a series of lessons as it will support them in consolidating their knowledge. It will also encourage the children to have a more informed discussion as they should always give reasons for placing a statement in a particular position. A topic for the statement could include: How can we save resources on our planet?

Jigsaw games

This method is described by Coultas (2007) and involves the children being placed in groups where they become an expert on one aspect of a subject. The area chosen could be a book such as 'The Firework Maker's Daughter' by Philip Pullman. Each group could focus on one character in the story. Then an expert from the group moves round all the other groups providing them with their knowledge. This allows a class to complete a task that requires information from each group.

Concept maps

This is a system used to structure planning so that connections can be made in thinking. The concept maps can be used at the start of a topic to support the organisation of research or at the end of the topic to make clear the information that has been obtained. The ideas for the concept maps were developed by Buzan (2003) and he provides a range of examples in his book 'Mind Maps for Kids'. In one example he takes a science topic on materials and places this in the middle of a page and from this he draws three lines which he labels solids, gases and liquids. From the liquid branch he continues to divide the line.

Similarities and differences

This activity is suggested by Fisher (2005) to support thinking skills through discussion. He states that 'the more children can think aloud in informal discussions the more they become responsible for formulating and refining their own ideas in the struggle to create meaning and patterns from their own experiences' (Fisher 2005 page 184). He suggests using two or more pictures or objects and asking the children to suggest something that is different or similar about the objects and discussing their answers. The pictures or objects could be different fruits, animals or trees. The pictures could show change over a period of time and the children encourage to observe and discuss the changes if necessary prompted by questions.

Learning Outcomes Review

This chapter has explored what is meant by the term thinking skills. It has also considered your role in developing strategies and resources to support children develop good thinking skills which will help to support their cross-curricular learning.

Self-assessment questions

1. Give ten reasons why you consider it important to teach thinking skills.
2. Plan an activity for developing the following three kinds of thinking a) critical thinking, b) creative thinking and c) caring or co-operative thinking. State when opportunities for each kind will be taking place, which areas of the curriculum will be covered and the year group for which your lesson is planned.

Further Reading

http://thinkingtogether.educ.cam.ac.uk/
This is the website for the 'Thinking Together' project that uses a dialogue-based approach to thinking and learning from the University of Cambridge. It contains downloadable material for teachers and provides information regarding books and useful links.

Clough, N. (2012) Using children's talk as a basis for reflective practice. In Hansen, A. (ed) *Reflective learning and teaching in primary schools*. London: Learning Matters.
This chapter helps you to develop your practice that is based in the literature of pupil talk for learning.

Buzan, T. (2003) *Mind Maps for Kids*. London: Thorson.
Tony Buzan explains, in a very visual way, a range of methods to support children organise their ideas and thinking.

De Bono, E. (2009) *Six Thinking Hats*. London: Penguin. edwdebono@msn.com
This book and website provide more information about the six thinking hats and how they can be used to structure children's thinking.

Fisher, R. (1996) *Stories for Thinking*. Oxford: Nash Pollock.

Fisher, R. (1997) *Games for Thinking*. Oxford: Nash Pollock.

Fisher, R. (1997) *Poems for Thinking*. Oxford: Nash Pollock.
Robert Fisher's books provide a range of resources to support children develop thinking and learning skills.

Mooney, C. (2000) *An introduction to Dewey, Montessori, Erickson, Piaget and Vygotsky*. USA: Redleaf Press.
This book gives a brief introduction to the theories of Piaget and Vygotsky which have influenced the way thinking skills have developed more recently.

Wallace, B. (ed.) (2009) (Guest editors: June Maker and Bob Zimmerman) *Thinking Actively in a Social Context: Theory and Practice*. Kent, UK.
A full analysis of the TASC Framework with examples of school practice at all phases of education. More information about TASC Framework can be found on tasc@sheffield.gov.uk

References

Adey, P., Roberton A. and Venville, G. (2001) *Let's think! A Programme for Developing/thinking in Five and Six year olds*. London: NFERNelson.

Alexander, R.J. (2008) *Towards dialogic teaching* (4th edition). York: Dialogos.

Bruner J. (1966) *The Process of Education*. Cambridge, MA: Harvard University Press (25th edition 1999).

Buzan, T. (2003) *Mind Maps for Kids*. London: Thorson.

Coultas V. (2007) *Constructive Talk in Challenging Classrooms*. Abingdon: Routledge.

De Bono, E. (2009) *Six Thinking Hats*. London: Penguin.

Department for Education and Employment (DfEE) (1999) *The National Curriculum: handbook for teachers in England. Key stages 1 and 2*. London HMSO.

Department for Education and Employment (DfEE) (2011) *The framework for the National Curriculum. A report by the Expert Panel for the National Curriculum review*. London: DfE.

Dewey, J. (1993) *How we Think*. Lexington, MA: D.C. Heath.

Donaldson, M. (1978) *Children's Minds*. London: Fontana.

Ennis, R. (2001) Goals for a critical thinking curriculum and its assessment. In A. Costa (ed) *Developing Minds: A Resources book for teaching thinking* (3rd edition). London: Association for Supervision and Curriculum Development.

Fisher, R. (2005) *Teaching children to think* (2nd edition). Cheltenham: Nelson Thornes College, Columbia University. New York: AMS Press.

Hattie, J. (2008) *Visible learning. A synthesis of over 800 meta-analyses relating to achievement*. London: Routledge Education.

Lipman, M. (2003) *Thinking in Education*. Cambridge University Press.

Mooney, C. (2000) *An introduction to Dewey, Montessori, Erickson, Piaget and Vygotsky*. USA: Redleaf Press.

Robinson, K. (2001) *Out of our minds: Learning to be Creative.* Oxford: Capstone.

Smith, J. (2010) *Talk, Thinking and Philosophy in the Primary Classroom.* Exeter: Learning Matters Ltd.

Taggart, G., Ridley, K., Rudd, P. and Benefield, P. (2005) *Thinking skills in the early years: A Literature Review.* London: NFERNelson.

Vygotsky, L. (1986) *Thought and Language.* (Revised edition). Kozulin A. Cambridge, MA: MIT Press.

Wallace, B. (ed.) (2009) (Guest editors: June Maker and Bob Zimmerman) *Thinking Actively in a Social Context: Theory and Practice.* Kent, UK.

PART 2:
INTRODUCTION

Part 2 moves beyond the focus of curriculum subjects to explore English in a wider context and across the school day. It recognises that English is much more than a lesson on the timetable or a contributor to other subjects. English is not only central to children's ability to access the curriculum; it is also the medium through which all the activities of school life and the school community will be communicated. In this context it is argued that valuable learning takes place through English. Part 2 also explores how children can continue to learn about English beyond timetabled lessons.

Part 2 considers how you, as a trainee teacher, will use English professionally and academically to be effective in your teaching role. Your own professional use of English is highlighted in the context of communicating with colleagues, parents and carers and in fulfilling your responsibilities in lesson planning, assessment and record keeping. The role of English subject leadership is considered with reference to policy development and the promotion of English within and beyond the curriculum. It is intended that you consider how you can use and develop your own English capability through your teaching and all that the role entails.

7. Teachers' wider roles: communication and assessment

Learning Outcomes

This chapter aims to help you to:

- understand the primary teacher's role in supplying objective, accurate, appropriate and succinct written and spoken communication;
- understand the use of English in communicating with parents and carers;
- understand the use of English in communicating with colleagues and fellow professionals;

- be able to describe the main sources of written assessment criteria for primary English;
- be able to evaluate examples of primary English planning and record keeping.

TEACHERS' STANDARDS

A teacher must:

2. **Promote good progress and outcomes by pupils**
- be accountable for pupils' attainment, progress and outcomes
- plan teaching to build on pupils' capabilities and prior knowledge
- guide pupils to reflect on the progress they have made and their emerging needs
- demonstrate knowledge and understanding of how pupils learn and how this impacts on teaching
- encourage pupils to take a responsible and conscientious attitude to their own work and study

5. **Adapt teaching to respond to the strengths and needs of all pupils**
- have a clear understanding of the needs of all pupils, including those with special educational needs; those of high ability; those with English as an additional language; those with disabilities; and be able to use and evaluate distinctive teaching approaches to engage and support them

6. **Make accurate and productive use of assessment**
- know and understand how to assess the relevant subject and curriculum areas, including statutory assessment requirements
- make use of formative and summative assessment to secure pupils' progress
- use relevant data to monitor progress, set targets, and plan subsequent lessons
- give pupils regular feedback, both orally and through accurate marking, and encourage pupils to respond to the feedback

7. **Fulfil wider professional responsibilities**
- take responsibility for improving teaching through appropriate professional development, responding to advice and feedback from colleagues communicate effectively with parents with regard to pupils' achievements and well-being

Introduction

Part 1 explored how children learn and use English in a cross-curricular approach. However, your own use of English has a broader context. This is the context of the wider role of the primary classroom teacher. It demands that you are a fluent, articulate and accurate English language user who reads avidly. Effective primary teachers can encourage in others a love of language, drama, reading and writing that transcends curriculum boundaries.

In addition to planning, teaching and assessment, class teachers are responsible for myriad pupil-related tasks. In essence, the vast majority of these tasks relate to teachers' accountability. The primary teacher is accountable to pupils, parents, the school's English co-ordinator, the head teacher and the local authority. They must account for the academic and social progress that children achieve in school. In turn, the government, via inspection bodies like Ofsted, closely monitors pupils' progress. How you use your own English language and literacy skills, when interacting with these people, can affect how they perceive and respond to you. This chapter discusses the role of English in each of these wider contexts. It is organised under two section headings.

1. Communication
2. Assessment

Communicating with parents

This part of the chapter considers the research that has made clear the importance of building good professional communication with parents and carers. It considers some of the initiatives successfully implemented in schools and considers strategies that support you in establishing home/school links.

Activity
Thinking about home/school links
In your time in school, you will have observed or been involved in a range of activities that support and develop contact with parents and carers. Use the headings below to write down what you have observed to encourage contact between parents and carers, the wider community and the school.

- Contact with parents and carers on an informal basis
- Formal contact during the school year to share information
- Participation in school events
- Participation in the work of the school i.e. membership of the PTA
- Links with the wider community

As you read this part of the chapter add to these headings.

....

Research Focus: Research into home/school links

Most successful schools encourage and promote a close partnership with parents and carers in the education of their children but until recently there was little evidence to support this practice. As the range of interventions to promote parental involvement has increased, more structured evaluation of these initiatives has established that parental involvement with the school can influence a child's educational attainment, behaviour and attendance at school.

The previous Government's strategy for encouraging home/school links was a focus in the White Paper Excellence in Schools (DfEE, 1997).Its aims remain the focus today. They are

- to provide parents with information
- to give parents a voice
- to encourage parental partnership with schools

The White Paper encouraged schools to review, develop and provide a more planned structure to their initiatives. The initiatives fell into five main areas.

- The development of parent governor roles.
- Involvement in the inspection process.
- The provision of annual reports and prospectuses.
- The requirement of home-school agreement.
- The provision of increasing amounts of information to parents.

Making successful home/school links

As a trainee teacher, you need to know the information available to support any whole-school initiative and so develop your own contact with parents. Your college audit on school experience will give you some guidance on activities in which you need to be involved. These might include meeting parents informally at the start or end of the school day, attending formal parents' evenings with your class teacher, attending PTA meetings and contributing to after school clubs and events. Each school will have its own environment and you will need to make your own assessments of the needs of the child within the context of the community and the family.

The study below will help you understand some of the research that has been carried out to support the theory that early intervention in establishing links between home and school has significant results in both academic achievement and the social behaviour of the child.

Research Focus: Research study

Hannon and Nutbrown (2001, p1) posed the question 'How can early years educators collaborate with parents to promote pre-school literacy development?' Their project, which ran for over a decade, was called Raising Early Achievement in Literacy (REAL). It focused on children with literacy attainments significantly below the national norms. Ten schools were involved in the project that involved establishing contact with parents and children in the 12–18 months before they started school. Activities to support this included home visits by teachers, special events on subjects of interest to the parents including information about the curriculum where opportunities were provided for informal and formal communication. This research asked parents to volunteer on the understanding they had a 50/50 chance of being allocated to the control group so the results of this research could be verified. The results of this study made clear that the focus group of children in the project made more literacy progress.

As a trainee teacher you need to consider how you develop your practice and make links with parents to support the children in your class to develop their literacy skills.

Case Study: Parents' evening

The following case study explores how Sarah, a newly qualified teacher in a Year 1 class, developed contact with the parents and carers in her class. The school was situated in a multicultural area of south London. During the first week of term, Sarah invited parents to an evening meeting. She explained that it was intended to demonstrate some of the resources and methods used for teaching reading. She felt that many families were keen to be involved in supporting their children, but were not confident in knowing how to do this. During the meeting Sarah demonstrated how ranges of resources were used for teaching phonics including phoneme fans, sound buttons and the interactive whiteboard. She explained how children were supported in their reading development through phonics, guided and shared reading, and she explained how this was organised in the classroom.

In a question and answer session Sarah discussed family support for reading at home. She demonstrated the reading journal and provided examples of journal entries that demonstrated a range of support strategies including discussion about the book. Sarah completed the evening by provided a list of books that contained a range of genres contain non-fiction and poetry books so that family members felt more confident in selecting future reading material. She had arranged for the local librarian to be at the meeting to speak to families. Communicating with parents gave parents the confidence and knowledge to work in partnership with school.

> ## Links to the National Curriculum
> The information Sarah gave to parents focused on the children's need to develop phonemic awareness and phonic knowledge. This included hearing, identifying, segmenting and blending phonemes in words, sounding out and naming the letters of the alphabet, linking sound and letter patterns, identifying syllables in words, recognising that the same sounds may have different spelling and that the same spellings may relate to different sounds. Sarah also linked the information she gave to families to the Letters and Sounds materials from the Department of Education (Department for Education and Skills, 2007).

Communicating with colleagues

This section of the chapter considers the use of English in communicating with colleagues in school. It is important that both oral and written communication between colleagues is carried out in a professional manner. How you use your own literacy skills when interacting with other school staff can influence how they perceive and respond to you. As you deal with colleagues, you must be aware of the best ways to communicate with them so that the children's best interests are served and that the adults' professional development is enhanced.

> ## Activity
> Consider the adults who assist in school. What were their roles? How much did they support the class teacher and children and what tasks did they undertake? Make a list of those occasions when you observed other adults either leading or supporting the learning of groups or individuals.

Professional dialogue

Many adults can contribute to pupils' progress in school. You may have encountered the work of peripatetic speech and language or occupational therapists, behavioural specialists and educational psychologists. Their remit is to undertake detailed assessments or deliver aspects of their expertise to children referred to their particular education or medical service. Educational professionals will often compile written reports that require information from you as the class teacher. Frank and honest discussions that will benefit the children's development will be necessary. Subjective and unsubstantiated comments from any party, including you, are to be avoided. Strict confidentiality is essential. If you are unsure, seek advice from more senior members of staff such as the Special Educational Needs Co-ordinator (SENCo), inclusion manager or head teacher.

Teamwork is essential to effective primary schools. Class teachers recognise the different roles carried out by in-class support staff. These include nursery nurses, teaching or learning support assistants or HLTAs. These members of staff work either on a 1:1 basis or by supporting small groups of children who have special educational needs (SEN). They may also work with children who have English as an additional language (EAL).

It is useful for teachers to consider how and when they will discuss the implementation of planned assessment, teaching and learning activities with support staff allocated to particular children. This will include the writing of formal reports. Manageability is a key aim. Some schools will have specific procedures and times for liaison and feedback. This may be at weekly meetings and at crucial times of the year such as before parents' evenings. Newly qualified and established members of staff all need to be aware of this schedule.

Research Focus: Working with HLTAs

Higher Level Teaching Assistants are experienced teaching assistants who plan and deliver learning activities under the direction of a teacher and assess, record and report on pupils' achievements and areas for development. They have a higher status in the school than other teaching or learning support assistants. To achieve this status, they are required to reach defined standards, established through the National Agreement between Government, local government employers and school workforce unions in 2003. Some HLTAs have subject-specific knowledge and skills that allow them to specialise their support. For example, Wilson et al.'s survey on the deployment and impact of HLTAs (TDA, 2007) commented on the improvements to pupil performance that many school leaders reported when they used mathematics HLTAs to help with individuals and groups of children. The survey also reported how leaders felt that HLTAs helped to reduce teacher workload; the role of many HLTAs as line managers to other teaching assistants was useful.

Case Study: An HLTA in Year 2

A newly qualified teacher, Katie, was pleased to learn that, following a school decision over the deployment of delegated resources, a child in her Year 2 class was to receive 10 hours of additional support from Marcus, an HLTA who had been working in the school for a number of years. The child was having difficulties in accessing the curriculum due to mild cerebral palsy. It resulted in poor gross and fine motor control, compounded by a visual impairment (astigmatism).The child was working well below age expectations and needed tasks and targets that were different from most of the children in the class. The support had been organised by the school's inclusion manager. Marcus would be supporting the child in class every morning during literacy and numeracy lessons.

It was important that Katie and Marcus were clear about the specific support that was needed for the child. Both had been involved in attending and contributing to

$\rightarrow$

a meeting when the child's most recent Individual Education Provision (IEP) was devised. This meeting involved the child's parents, so it allowed Katie and Marcus to meet them. They planned an informal fortnightly discussion of the child's progress in addition to the statutory termly review of the child's IEP.

Standardised formats for IEPs do not currently exist nationwide. Planned provision on the IEP should contain relevant, detailed short-term targets, evaluation of the targets and teaching strategies that are different from, or are in addition to, those in place for the rest of the class. All interested parties receive a final copy. The language used on the document must be accessible to all relevant parties. Acronyms or abbreviations need to be avoided or explained.

Katie's school also had a policy to discuss the document with the child. Specific, measurable, attainable, realistic and time-lined (SMART) targets had to be written so that the child understood them. For example, 'I will use a pencil grip and my writing slope to help me to keep all my handwriting letters on the line in the next ten pieces of writing'.

On each Thursday, Marcus received a copy of Katie's class literacy and numeracy planning. He planned and adapted activities to maximise the child's ability to integrate into each lesson. Katie recorded all adaptations on to her lesson planning. As is best practice, Marcus' planning was used as a working document with a section available for a bullet-pointed evaluation of each activity. He shared this every day with Katie so that they could discuss further necessary adaptations. In a lively classroom it was not always easy to have these discussions. The written feedback on the lesson plan enabled them to monitor the child's progress. This information was used to address the IEP targets.

Links to the National Curriculum

The National Curriculum statement for inclusion has three principles: the setting of suitable learning challenges, responding to pupils' diverse needs and overcoming potential barriers to learning and assessment of individuals and groups of pupils (DfEE, 1999). Katie and Marcus had a clear and manageable focus on planning and assessment, based on the child's learning needs. This was transferred to the IEP. Such classroom practice exemplifies a commitment to collaborative working.

Communicating with teachers

Many teachers comment on the positive side of having autonomy within their own classroom. Working as part of a team of teachers also has positive benefits. It is important to exploit opportunities to learn from experienced staff. Recognising more highly trained and experienced teachers as they impart their knowledge and skills is important. It shows that you value their developed understanding of teaching and learning. Effective and professional communication with them builds a collegiate atmosphere and promotes teamwork. For example, teachers who work in the same age phase often meet together to plan weekly lessons based on the same medium term planning. This allows for a consistency of approach and a sharing of resources.

Most schools hold a weekly staff meeting. At this meeting, day-to-day issues are discussed and training takes place. New school, local or national statutory or non-statutory initiatives on curriculum subjects or generic areas of education are often taught at this time. Maintained schools have to follow the National Curriculum and all related training initiatives. Whole staff training topics are largely determined by the school's action plan. Trainee teachers are often invited to staff meetings so that they feel part of the school community. For trainee teachers, it is best to go to any meeting prepared to take notes as part of your training or classroom practice. Ask for copies of any relevant handouts from the meetings. Do not be embarrassed to ask questions.

Policy writing

Policies require a high standard of written English. An effective curriculum area policy needs to be well structured and clearly written for its audience. It should contain:

- a rationale for the policy;
- clear aims;
- objectives linked to the Programmes of Study of the National Curriculum;
- possible teaching and learning strategies;
- resourcing;
- cross-curricular links;
- ICT links;
- implications for inclusion/SEN;
- assessment and monitoring procedures.

All staff, including newly appointed staff, need to be familiar with school policies and how their implementation. They are often discussed in staff meetings when they are updated or altered to suit changing circumstances. These important documents reflect the prevailing ethos of the school. They can relate to curriculum subjects or general issues such as admissions, child protection, behaviour management or special educational needs. Some documents are statutory. The governing body is legally bound to know the detail of some policies and to liaise with subject coordinators on their implementation. The current Government position on policies in maintained schools is accessible at, www.education.gov.uk/search/results?q=maintained+schools

As you progress through your teaching career, you may be involved in writing policy documents in your role as a curriculum co-ordinator.

Assessment, planning and record keeping

This part of the chapter offers an analytical argument for the collection and monitoring of school performance data. The first section explains how classroom planning and record keeping link to assessment as part of a cycle of teaching and learning. The second section gives some examples of different types of English assessment and record keeping across the curriculum. It shows how class teachers must adapt their use of English for each of these tasks. The final section considers how assessment and record keeping data inform the development of primary English teaching. It considers differences in the interpretation of data by different audiences. It notes how this affects the class teachers' preparation of it. The use of appropriate English in report writing for parents is included.

In the primary classroom, assessment takes three forms, diagnostic, summative or formative. Summative assessment is essentially testing, a snapshot of how the pupil performs with a standardised test according to the expected level for his age group or for the class to which he or she belongs. Formative assessment is ongoing assessment. This kind of assessment happens on a daily basis. It can take many forms such as through teacher questioning and observation. Specific English techniques such as reading running records and miscue analysis or an analysis of spelling and phonic errors, provide both formative and diagnostic data for the class teacher. Formative assessment allows the class teacher to see the progress of learning and to modify the teaching accordingly. Diagnostic assessment highlights specific difficulties with learning, the most serious of which will require assessment from an educational psychologist.

The teaching, learning and assessment cycle

Assessment, planning and pupils' learning are part of a continuous cycle that has pupil performance at its heart. It considers pupils' previous knowledge of the subject in addition to their formal assessments. Central to this approach to teaching is a deep understanding of the required levels of academic achievement for each age group. For primary school teachers it also includes developmental knowledge of what this achievement looks like across the range of primary schooling. In primary English, this includes knowledge of the statutory assessment frameworks of the National Curriculum as well as knowledge of the natural developmental progression of language and literacy in children. It presupposes an ability to synthesise and to present the salient aspects of this knowledge for pupils, for parents, for the English coordinator, for the local authority and for Ofsted. All teachers utilise the same process for teaching and assessing pupils' learning.

Activity

Linking assessment to planning

Look at the generic half term medium term plan for Year 3 English in Table 7.1 below. Make a copy of the table and in the two blank columns, note specific assessment opportunities that come before and after each unit of work. They will be a mixture of summative and formative assessments.

Pre assessment opportunities	Teaching weeks	Unit theme	Learning Objectives	Spelling and grammar	Shared texts	Suggested outcomes	Cross-curri-cular links	Post assessment opportunities
	1	Stories with familiar setting	Use beginning middle and end in narrative writing	Prefixes Sight word check up Compound sentences	Flat Stanley	Re-write sections of story in own words to make into class book	Art	
	2	Stories with familiar setting	Use beginning middle and end in narrative writing	Antonyms and prefixes	The Day the Smells Went Wrong	Write story board of own version of the story	Art	
	3	Stories with familiar setting	Empathise with characters and debate moral dilemmas	Prefixes, compound and simple sentences	Harry's Dog	Write letter from Harry to his dog	Drama	
	4	Myths and legends	Use play script layout accurately	Revision week	The Unicorn Dream	Perform improvisation of scene from book	History	
	5	Myths and legends	Use play script layout accurately	Y as vowel Science topic words Sentence expansion	Disney film: Robin Hood	Improvisation of scene from film, written by pupils	History	

Table 7.1 Linking assessment to planning in Year 3

This activity will have alerted you to the need to consider the assessed needs of the pupils in planning as part of the teaching, learning and assessment cycle. A number of assessment opportunities are feasible. For example, you may have noted the need for summative spelling and phonic assessments or writing targets derived from assessed pieces of writing using National Curriculum attainment criteria. These are taken from across the curriculum. Formatively, you may have noted various opportunities for observation throughout the school day.

Links to the National Curriculum
KS2: En2: 1, 2, 4, 8a, 8f. En3: 2, 3,4a, 4d, 7c, 9a, 12. The planning in this activity links to writing. Transcription and composition in the writing processes of phonics, grammar and composition are addressed each week within the context of shared reading of real texts.

Assessment and record keeping in the classroom

The assessment and recording of primary English occurs in a number of ways. Each method demands a different literacy and language skill set from the class teacher. Class teachers need to have an accurate understanding of each pupil's progress in the four modes of English. This recorded data looks different according to its summative or formative purpose. For example, reading assessment for the class teacher means weekly guided reading records, assessed, teacher assessments of National Curriculum attainment levels, Standard Attainment Test scores [SATS], home-school reading journals, and school library records of pupils' borrowed books as well as a record of pupils' achievement in individual lessons. It may also include phonic assessments and results from diagnostic reading assessments for individual children. The management and recording schedules for this data differs. While some schools require corporate documentation, others allow teachers to develop schedules to suit their own working styles. However, even with relative flexibility it is important for the trainee and NQT to consider the following.

- Manageability: are recording and assessment procedures workable in the long-term?
- Comprehension: can others, such as supply teachers, student teachers and colleagues, understand and use them efficiently?
- How do they assist with end of year report writing?
- How well do they indicate the detail of pupils' different abilities and attainment?
- How do they inform future planning?

Using and presenting data

The Government uses data as evidence for the effect of National Curriculum policies. It provides a national, if controversial picture of national trends. They can be viewed at the Department of Education's research and statistics site (http://www.education.gov.uk/rsgateway). Although the independent Cambridge Review (Alexander, 2010), has questioned the validity of these test results, schools continue to be judged, at least in part, by their test and examination data.

In schools, class teachers simultaneously collect formative and summative assessment data. The RAISEonline (Ofsted and Department for Education, 2011), package is currently in use for summative data.

English coordinators use formative data to check whole school parity of provision, continuity and progression. This monitoring role involves checking the links between teachers' assessment, planning and teaching across the year groups and of English use across the curriculum. It may include the selection of work samples.

Local authorities may ask for summative reading scores, school English action plans and examples of pupils' work.

Finally, parents need to know, succinctly and clearly, how their child is performing in relation to other children in that age group and in relation to individual progress. Parents also need to know how they can help their child to progress. In speaking and writing reports to parents, it is important to strike a balance between providing enough data and sufficient practical suggestions. Excessive amounts of professional jargon or subjective comments are not useful. Most schools have a specific format for report writing.

Activity

List examples of the class teacher's writing assessment and record keeping data. How is this information reported to parents, to Ofsted, to the English coordinator and to the local authority?

How does the class teacher's use of written and spoken English change?

What professional demands does this make on the primary class teacher?

A number of different audiences use achievement data, gathered by the class teacher, for a variety of different purposes. It is the class teacher's responsibility to gather and present data in the most appropriate format for each body.

Learning Outcomes Review

This chapter has explored the use of English in teachers' wider roles. It has given a broad range of examples of the adaptation of English for different audiences. Throughout your classroom career, you will be required to account for the academic and social progress of pupils in your classroom and at school. This demands teamwork and a level of professional English to know and meet the demands of each member of that team. Parents, colleagues, local authorities and Ofsted are part of this team. Establishing sound subject and pedagogical knowledge, key techniques and routines will enable this process to run smoothly and consistently.

Self-assessment questions

1. Consider the information and support needed for parents or carers when a child joins a class during the school year.
2. Consider the key differences in reporting assessment data to Ofsted, to parents and to colleagues.
3. List the different literacy-linked policies that a school may choose to devise for teaching and learning.

Further Reading and Resources

These resources and readings provide a perspective of the wider role of primary English teaching and learning.

Martin, T. and Waters, M. (2007) *Coordinating English at Key Stage 2*. London: Routledge.

Gill, N. and Tyrrell, J. (2000) *Coordinating English at Key Stage 1*. London: Routledge.

National Standard Attainment Test data can be viewed at http://www.education.gov.uk/rsgateway

References

Alexander, R. (ed) (2010) *Children, their world, their education: Final report and recommendations of the Cambridge Primary Review*. London: Routledge.

Department for Education and Employment (DfEE) (1999) *The National Curriculum: handbook for teachers in England. Key Stages 1 and 2*. London: HMSO.

Department for Education and Skills (2007) Letters and Sounds: Principles and practice of high quality phonics, Ref: 00281-2007BKT-EN. London: DFES.

DfEE (1997) The Excellence in Schools. White Paper.

Hannon, P. and Nutbrown, C. (2001) Outcomes for children and Parents of an Early Literacy Education Parental Involvement Programme. Paper presented at the British Educational Research Association Annual Conference. Leeds.

National Standard Attainment Test data can be viewed at http://www.education.gov.uk/rsgateway

Ofsted and Department for Education (2011) *About Raiseonline* (Publication). Retrieved 3.2.2011: www.raiseonline.org/About.asp.

Wilson, R., Sharp, C., Shuayb, M., Kendall, L., Wade, P. and Easton, C. (2007) *Research into the Deployment and Impact of Support Staff Who have Achieved HLTA Status*. London: TDA.

8. The role of primary English in researching teaching and learning

Learning Outcomes

This chapter aims to help you to:

- identify the key national and international journals for primary English research;
- consider the importance of the teaching and learning in the four modes of English across the primary curriculum;
- describe the cycle of governmental priorities for primary English in UK schools;
- describe the significance of primary English research for raising standards in teaching and learning across the primary curriculum.

TEACHERS' STANDARDS

A teacher must:

8. Fulfil wider professional responsibilities

- take responsibility for improving teaching through appropriate professional development, responding to advice and feedback from colleagues communicate effectively with parents with regard to pupils' achievements and well-being
- develop effective professional relationships with colleagues, knowing how and when to draw on advice and specialist support

3. Demonstrate good subject and curriculum knowledge

- demonstrate an understanding of and take responsibility for promoting high standards of literacy, articulacy and the correct use of standard English, whatever the teacher's specialist subject
- have a secure knowledge of the relevant subject(s) and curriculum areas, foster and maintain pupils' interest in the subject, and address misunderstandings
- demonstrate a critical understanding of developments in the subject and curriculum areas, and promote the value of scholarship

Introduction

This chapter concentrates on the process of researching teaching and learning in cross-curricular primary English. It begins by describing a generic educational research process with cross-curricular examples from current primary English research. The second half of the chapter provides an historical insight into the concurrence between raising educational standards in primary literacy levels and patterns of primary English research. The chapter concludes with some practical suggestions for developing your primary English subject knowledge as you progress through your NQT year and beyond.

In the previous chapters, cross-curricular English has been largely considered from a school perspective. However, it is important that you also consider your continuing professional development (CPD) from a wider perspective. In the state sector of education in the United Kingdom, CPD does not currently automatically link to compulsory refresher courses or to salary, with the exception of performance related pay and Standard Attainment Testing (SATS). This is unlike other professions, for example in nursing. Instead, teachers engage in annual appraisals that link to bespoke patterns of CPD. Usually appraisal considers the needs of the pupils, the school and the long-term career structure of the appraised teacher. Different patterns of CPD operate according to individual circumstances. Some CPD has a compulsory element, such as that for newly qualified teachers and those aiming for headship.

Researching teaching and learning is one aspect of CPD that has the potential to have a simultaneous impact on you as the trainee and/or class teacher, the children and the school. Positive classroom impact particularly occurs if research combines reflective diagnosis and practical solutions previously identified by the participants themselves. Unique research, that can be generalised, may ultimately influence primary education as a whole.

The process of researching teaching and learning begins in initial teacher training. Broadly speaking, it usually involves you in a cycle of reflection, practice, evaluation and re-practising of the teaching and learning process. Your tutors, peers, school-based colleagues and pupils assist with this process. In the context of cross-curricular primary English, this implies looking at teaching and learning issues within and across the four modes of English: speaking, listening, reading and writing. The four English modes can have an impact on pupils' achievement across the whole of the primary curriculum.

Terminology

A number of technical terms appear in this chapter.

- **Teaching** is the craft of the teacher; the pedagogy; its science and its principles.
- **Learning** is that which occurs because of teaching and/or because of the learning environment. Sometimes learning does not occur or it occurs in spite of the teaching or of the environment in which it has taken place. Spontaneous learning can be beneficial and long lasting but such incidental learning is not always fruitful.
- **The four modes of English** refer to reading, writing, speaking and listening.
- **Meta-cognition** describes the pupils' knowledge of their own thought and the factors that influence their thinking. In the same way, as explicit mathematical vocabulary enables the pupil to describe mathematical phenomenon, meta-cognitive thinking in primary English enables the pupil to describe the processes of writing or reading. This explicit knowledge gives

the pupil tools to address comprehension, grammar and spelling. This includes knowledge of how writing is adapted for different audiences and purposes.

- **Continuing professional development** (CPD) describes the inset training undertaken by professional teachers.
- **Synthetic phonics** describes how pupils segment and blend from taught letters and phonemes.
- **Whole language** describes work that grew from an approach developed by Ken Goodman in the 1960s. Whole language included the notion that pupils could decode words by looking at the context in which they were written.
- **Analytical phonics** describes the process of looking at sections of words and at patterns in sounds and words. It includes the decoding of words based on the initial sound (onset) and the alliterative ending of the word (rime), for example: c/at.

Action research for learning and teaching

Action research is a broad term that encompasses a vast range of research methods that impact on your knowledge, understanding and practice. Ideally, action research bridges the gap between research and practice by making teaching practice more reflective and in doing so, by improving the impact of the teaching process on pupils' learning achievements.

In order to illustrate the impact action research can have on your teaching and children's learning, read the case study below. Jack's experience illustrates the impact of researching teaching and learning during initial teacher training.

Case Study: Educational research to support initial teacher training

Jack was a PGCE trainee studying a Master's level module called 'Supporting Teaching and Learning'. The purpose of the assignment was to distinguish and apply key teaching and learning theories in a practical classroom context, with supporting data.

Jack had a keen interest in the important debate between the merits of synthetic or analytical approaches to teaching phonics (Rose, 2006). He was particularly interested in understanding how these approaches looked across Key Stage 1 and Key Stage 2 classes. He began his assignment by posing a key question: What are the similarities and differences between a synthetic and an analytic approach to phonics in primary school? Jack was placed in a high performing school. He completed a small research study to answer his key question. He examined the Key Stage 1 and Key Stage 2 phonic and spelling curricula, pupils' written work and the documentation of their phonic progress. He mapped the key elements of the

→

synthetic and analytic phonic approaches that he had found, and discovered that keys to success, with both approaches, were the systematic and rapid teaching of phonemes, along with a heavy emphasis on reading for meaning and pleasure.

Jack found that his research improved his own teaching and understanding of the place of phonics in the process of becoming a life-long reader. It also provided his school with evidence to pinpoint their success in choosing to use a mix of approaches to phonic teaching.

An overview of an action research process for teaching and learning

This section presents one action research model for a process of researching learning and teaching involving eight stages. It is important for you to see that much of your day-to-day conversations with peers and colleagues, coursework and reading already uses many of the skills that more formal action research requires. The key difference between the ongoing role of being a (trainee) teacher and being an action researcher is that in the latter you are far more systematic in your approach.

In the model presented and discussed here, each stage refines the research question.

1. Formulating a research question

2. Preliminary discussion with colleagues

3. Literature review

4. Modify initial question

5. Select research procedures

6. Select data analysis procedures

7. Carry out project

8. Interpretation of the data and dissemination of findings

(Adapted from Cohen et al., 2005, pp 235–236)

Formulating a research question

Research questions spring from a desire to address particular needs in the real classroom. Effective teachers are constantly striving to improve the impact of their work. Effective teachers of primary English have been found to have particular qualities that enable them to question, modify and evaluate their teaching in this way.

Research Focus

In 2001, a group of distinguished educational researchers set out to pinpoint the qualities of the most effective primary English teachers (Wray et al., 2002). In this study the research team, based on a range of data, identified 228 effective primary English teachers. Data included their pupils' learning gains. Their professional practice, educational belief systems and subject knowledge were compared to an equal number of teachers without the necessary data to be rated as effective primary English teachers.

Amongst a number of key findings, effective primary English teachers were characterised by extensive knowledge of the English language and of literacy acquisition. Although it was not always obvious in the classroom context, this extensive knowledge enabled them to make the purpose of English very explicit and therefore very relevant to the pupils in their charge. For example, aspects of grammar were rarely taught as discrete items. Instead, they were integral to the writing or speaking and listening process. Shared reading and writing were commonly used to achieve this. The research of Wray and his colleagues is also useful for examining the effectiveness of your own practice. It is discussed in more detail in the second part of this chapter.

Preliminary discussion with colleagues

Preliminary discussions with colleagues enable you to identify common patterns of pupils' behaviour or common educational issues outside of the classroom. At this stage, it is also useful to see if existing teachers have already expressed similar areas of concern. The annual 'What's Hot' survey, from the International Reading Association, lists the current areas of academic concern from a large cross-section of North American primary and secondary teachers (Cassidy et al., 2010). The British equivalent is produced annually by the National Literacy Trust (e.g. National Literacy Trust, 2009). These two surveys are useful barometers of English teachers' real classroom concerns. Other barometers of primary English concerns in the UK are the British government funded reports produced by the Office for Standards in Education (Ofsted).

Literature review

The literature review enables you to develop knowledge of existing research related to your research question. At this stage, it is useful to develop a systematic process for searching and recording details of references. The use of electronic referencing software, such as Endnote, is recommended. When using search engines on electronic databases it is important to be systematic in recording search strings of key words. This will alleviate much repetition at the later stages of a project. Finally, note taking is essential at each stage of the literature review. It is useful to develop notes that simultaneously feed into the original research question, review and summarise the key features of the articles, reports, or book sections.

The lists below provide essential starting points for your literature review.

Peer reviewed journals particular to primary English include:
- Reading Research Quarterly
- Literacy
- English in Education
- Journal of Research in Reading

Peer reviewed journals that contain primary English matters include:
- British Journal of Special Education
- Remedial and Special Education
- Educational Research (NFER)

Professional journals include:
- The Reading Teacher
- English 4-11
- NATE Classroom

Government funded and independent research bodies in the United Kingdom include:
- The Office for Standards in Education (Ofsted)
- The National Federation for Educational Research (NFER)
- The National Literacy Trust (NLT)
- The Centre for Literacy in Primary Education (CLPE)

Activity

In order to illustrate the initial process of finding links between primary research ideas, identify the common strands of research between the most recent editions of the listed surveys, journals and research bodies in the grid below. The first one has been done for you.

Research references	Common areas of primary English research													
	Reading motivation													
'What's Hot?' survey in IRA, USA	✓													
'What's Hot?' survey in NLT, UK	✓													
Reading Research Quarterly														
Literacy	✓													
The Reading Teacher														
Ofsted's annual report for primary schools	✓													
National Literacy Trust	✓													

Table 8.1 Discovering research perspectives in primary English

> The completed grid will allow you to begin to see the topicality and justification for your research question and to begin to identify current research trends in that area.

Modify initial question

The literature review enables modification of your research question. This may entail scaling down the question to link more closely with the aims of your research. In teaching and learning research, this often means linking your research to measurable outcomes. It is at this stage that decisions on the type of research procedures usually occur.

Select research procedures

Research procedures are usually defined as qualitative, quantitative or mixed methods approaches. In the past educational research was littered with arguments for the exclusive use of each approach. Literacy researchers have called for a truce in these so called 'paradigm wars', in order to engage the class teacher in practical research based solutions to everyday teaching and learning problems in literacy (Dillon et al., 2004).

Your selection of research procedures is as much dependent upon the opportunities provided by the university and by school experience as it is upon knowledge of different research procedures. In our experience, most trainees undertake some type of action research using case study or mixed-methods approaches.

Select data analysis procedures

It is useful to identify the process of data analysis in order to ensure that sufficient time and resources are available before any data is collected. It is also very important to ensure that the results truly represent the findings from the study. In particular, it is important not to attribute causality from data trends. You must also be aware of the dangers associated with generalising from the results of small samples.

Carry out project

In carrying out the project, it is useful to set a timescale in order to ensure sufficient opportunities to complete the work. It is also important to ensure that all ethical approvals and permissions for proposed research are gained. Each university has research ethics procedures and committees. Course tutors will advise you of how to fulfil these responsibilities.

Interpretation of the data and dissemination of findings

The interpretation of the data involves analysis of the results and its links to existing research or theory from the literature review. Dissemination of the results is likely to form part of your formal assessment. In practice, it should also inform your own academic skills, your teaching and the academic outcomes of the pupils in your charge.

In summary, an interpretation of the data means a description of the research results and of new knowledge that has been learned. Although this might be the endpoint in formally assessed work, it is important that you begin to use and apply the new knowledge you have learned in future contexts where appropriate.

Raising literacy standards and primary English research: an historical perspective

The second part of this chapter provides an historical insight into the concurrence between raising educational standards in primary literacy levels and patterns of primary English research. In doing so, it illustrates the key features of effective cross-curricular primary English and literacy teaching.

Activity
Effective teachers of literacy appear to possess distinctive knowledge and skills. Use the grid (Table 8.2 on page 134) to compare and contrast the evidence for effective primary English teaching in the 2011 Ofsted report, *Excellence in English: What we can learn from 12 outstanding schools* (Office for Standards in Education, 2011) and in *Teaching Literacy Effectively in the Primary School* (Wray et al., 2002).

The previous activity may have caused you to reflect on the quality of your own teaching with texts read and written by pupils across the curriculum. It will have allowed you to draw out key pedagogical features that will facilitate improved English and literacy learning across the curriculum. These are as follows.

- Reading and writing for meaning that separates grammar, spelling and comprehension
- Reading and writing for a real purpose
- Reading for pleasure
- Personal choice
- Differentiation based on cyclical assessment
- Learning challenge
- Active learning
- Shared texts across the curriculum

An historical perspective of primary English research

In the United Kingdom, standards of literacy and numeracy have been closely monitored since the beginnings of state funded education. In Victorian times, educational standards linked to grants determined by exam results, as the following extract from a school inspection report in 1889 shows.

Wray et al. 2002 Teaching Literacy Effectively in the Primary School	Ofsted 2011 Excellence in English: What we can learn from 12 outstanding schools	Common Element	Contrasting Element
Decoding, spelling and phonics are taught in a rigorous and systematic way that shows pupils why these methods are useful	A rigorous and systematic approach to teaching phonic knowledge and skills that adds to successful reading, spelling and writing		
They are very specific about how phonics, spelling, high frequency words, grammar and comprehension contribute to the derivation of meaning from text	Innovative curricula, that is tailor made to meet pupils' needs		
'Shared' texts are a key feature of all work with reading and writing text	Subject leaders provide a shared and coherent vision of the place of English across the curriculum		
They possess robust philosophies about how English and literacy should be taught	Improve teaching and learning through collaboration		
They have excellent procedures for monitoring and assessing pupil progress and for using the information to adapt teaching methods	Equal pupil access to the curriculum through adequate differentiation		
They emphasise the function of English and literacy. Therefore discrete skills like grammar are rarely taught in isolation	Empowering pupils to learn through the choice and challenge of learning		
	Reading for pleasure has a high profile across the curriculum and school		
	Apply English across the curriculum		
They have considerable experience of giving and receiving CPD. They have been or are literacy co-ordinators in school	Reflection and evaluation of teaching and learning is the norm		
They have extensive knowledge of the English language and literacy teaching, although not always in a state seen in a teaching context	Boys perform as well as girls. Learning is active		

Table 8.2 Identifying effective English teaching across the primary curriculum

In the senior section, the general tone is marred by the lack of life and interest in the girls. For English there is great hesitation that any grant at all will be recommended. The sixth standard is the only class that exudes any appearance of progress in this subject. In the other classes, grammar is unspeakably bad. Unless more rational work can be done in that subject any pretence of teaching ought to be given up.

(BBC, 2011)

Today educational standards continue to be monitored by the government. Research into teaching and learning is frequently a mix of ideas from educational psychology and sociology along with educational philosophy. Much primary English research focuses on understanding how reading and writing develop in mainstream pupils and in those with special educational needs. It seeks to uncover optimal conditions to promote educational attainment. This knowledge sits alongside specialist subject knowledge. In the context of primary English, this means an in-depth knowledge of children's literature, language and literacy. Educational research is undertaken by the government and by independent researchers. Some researchers act as governmental advisors.

Activity

Look at the timeline of examples of primary English research into the development of reading (Table 8.3 on page 136). Identify the trends in primary English reading research and government initiative and reports. Some are done for you. What are the implications for future teaching and learning research?

The previous activity provides some insight into how reading research links to policy initiatives and vice versa. It may also have caused you to consider the place of evidence-based reforms in primary English education.

Completing the table will have highlighted areas that encompass the four modes of English. Your effective research into teaching and learning in cross-curricular primary English involves both recognising and addressing these overarching themes in the practical classroom situations.

In the following case study, a trainee teacher uses her knowledge of current English research to enhance the research skills of Year 6 pupils, thus raising pupils' writing attainment.

Case Study: Developing research skills in Year 6

Jane was a BA, QTS, third year trainee on her final school experience in Year 6. The class had been studying the Second World War. Her class teacher mentor had asked Jane to address the development of research skills among the pupils in the class. Jane began by setting a piece of homework that required the pupils to write a report to explain child evacuation. When Jane collected the homework in, she found that the majority of the class had cut and pasted their descriptions of child

→

Date	Reading research	British governmental initiatives and reports	Trend	Possible implication for future cross-curricular English teaching and learning research in reading
1950s	Deficit model of reading pedagogy focussing upon the struggling reader	1944 Education Act & 11+ testing		How has the reading deficit of struggling readers changed?
1960+	Psycholinguistics promotes natural language development. Piagetian principles encourage 'discovery learning'. Chomsky theorises the Language Acquisition Device (Chomsky, 1965)	1967 The Plowden Report	Reading and language development are implicit	
1970s +	Information processing model emphasises a meta-cognitive approach to reading acquisition, the diagnosis and remediation of struggling readers	1975 The Bullock Report	Raising standards of reading to fulfil society's needs. No one method of teaching reading rules	
1980s	The Whole Language approach to reading acquisition evolves. Stanovich describes the 'Matthew Effect' (Stanovich, 1986): reading large amounts equals reading success	1981 Special Educational Needs Reform Act		How much does pupils' implicit and explicit knowledge of language effect their English development?
1990s	Active involvement of the reader, guided and shared reading appears. Assessment for/of learning debate in the UK (Black and Wiliam, 1998). Reading motivation declines	1990 First incarnation of a National Curriculum 1998 The National Literacy Strategy SATS	How does the social demographic and reading ethos of the school affect reading achievement?	
2000s	Decoding reading research develops to examine optimal processes for rapid reading acquisition. International PISA and PIRLS surveys show declines in reading motivation suggesting meta-cognition and reading motivation account for 25 per cent of variance in reading attainment	2006 Primary National Strategy (PNS) 2006 Rose Review 2011 Excellence in English: What we can learn from 12 outstanding schools 2011 PNS closes	Merits of analytical or synthetic phonics. Reading motivation. Differentiation and continuity. PNS includes speaking and listening	

Table 8.3 Comparing research, policy and practice in primary reading

evacuation from the internet. She knew this because the writing was disjointed. It did not relate to the level of writing or reading that the pupils were capable of in the class, nor were the pupils capable of answering related questions or of presenting their research orally except by reading their reports aloud verbatim.

Jane knew from her knowledge of National Curriculum levelling assessment that reading ability in Year 6 was strongly linked to reading comprehension and pupils' ability to interrogate texts. She also knew from research that effective literacy teachers encouraged reading choice and a relevant purpose for reading. Both would enhance pupils' reading motivation.

Using this knowledge Jane reset the evacuation homework. Instead of asking all pupils to write a report, Jane set the task of interpreting their research by presenting it in a range of text forms. The forms included poems, adventure stories, letters, posters, persuasive and discussion texts. She called this a 'genre exchange'. She asked for all homework to be presented in longhand.

The second set of homework gave Jane a real insight into the pupils' research, handwriting and presentation abilities. Not only did it demonstrate who could synthesise new knowledge but it also gave Jane an understanding of which writing genres were most secure. On their feedback sheets, the pupils commented on their enjoyment of being able to choose how to present their research in a creative way.

Developing English subject knowledge

All primary class teachers are required to update their subject knowledge as well as their knowledge of teaching and learning. Primary English knowledge is extended by understanding fundamental elements of effective primary English teaching, discussed in the previous section. Six further practices are suggested to ensure that such basic principles remain current.

Children's literature

It is important to read children's literature as part of your regular adult reading repertoire. Enthusiastic teachers, who are avid readers, are a model for primary children to emulate. Children's literature is the basis for good quality shared reading and writing across the curriculum. It is also the basis of motivating your pupils to become lifelong readers. Instigating a love of reading is part of the primary teacher's responsibility. As well as providing models of writing, being an avid reader of children's books will enable you as a teacher, to expand your pupils' creativity because you can choose or recommend texts to read in class. Wide reading can free you from teaching with unsuitable, outdated or poor examples of literature. Poor examples may include exclusive use of decontextualised text extracts that are a feature of some primary literacy schemes.

Unfortunately, a growing body of research suggests that trainees and teachers know less and less children's literature. As a result, teachers cannot recommend books or excite their pupils to read for pleasure. However, when teachers are reintroduced to the joys of children's literature it can transform pupils' motivation to read independently. Pupils become part of a reading community, where the purposes of reading for pleasure become apparent and relevant (Cremin et al., 2008; Cremin et al., 2009).

Working across key stages

Understanding primary English entails recognising pupils' literacy achievement at a developmental level as well as the required curriculum for each year group. Observing, teaching, planning and marking work from different year groups will allow you to see what English progression looks like. An insight into other year groups enables the trainee and the class teacher to plan each teaching and learning step into the next academic year. This awareness is of particular importance in the transition classes between key stages.

Knowledge of learning strategies for dyslexic pupils

Dyslexic pupils are an important consideration. *'Ten percent (10%) of the British population are dyslexic; 4% severely so. Dyslexia is identified as a disability as defined in the Equality Act 2010'* (BDA www.bdadyslexia.org.uk). Early formal diagnosis can be of real benefit to the child because it can relieve frustration and begin the process of learning the strategies that will help the child to access the curriculum. Trainees should observe the current arrangements for dyslexic pupils in their placement schools. Organisations like the British Dyslexia Association provide resources, training and support for schools and families. Additional certificated training in this area is a consideration for those teachers who wish to specialise. Basic courses will also provide the trainee and the practising teacher with the necessary skills for the day-to-day teaching of dyslexic pupils.

Knowledge of learning strategies for EAL pupils

Pupils for whom English is an additional language are also an important consideration although the immediate impact of this kind of pupil is likely to depend on your placement school. Learning English as an additional language in an English speaking school can present a number of challenges both for the pupils and for their teachers. These have been outlined in an earlier chapter. Organisations like the National Association for Language Development in the Curriculum provide resources, training and research into this area.

English teaching associations

Keeping up to date with current trends and courses in primary English is often best managed through membership of a national organisation. One of the oldest and largest in the UK is the United Kingdom Literacy Association. Organisations like these provide a whole range of courses, conferences, professional journals and teaching magazines. A regional network of UKLA members is in operation.

English resources

Every year a wealth of new teaching resources are published in addition to reading schemes, library books and specialist consumables. Specialist English resources can be found in many generic catalogues that are available in school. One simple way of updating your knowledge of English classroom resources is to browse these catalogues. Some local educational authorities loan out these materials from teachers' centres. The school librarian is another great resource. Cultivating a professional relationship with the local children's library and your local bookshop is also a useful strategy for extending English knowledge.

Learning Outcomes Review

This chapter has explored the role of English in researching teaching and learning. It has given a broad range of examples of cross-curricular English research with a key focus on teaching and learning. Throughout your classroom career, you will be required to increase your professional skills as a recipient of in-service training and through action research of your own classroom practice. Establishing a basic knowledge of the action research process, together with pupil's literature and the four modes of English, will enable you to develop your teaching and learning of English from a strong foundation of secure subject knowledge.

Self-assessment questions

1. Provide at least three reasons why primary classroom teachers should use peer reviewed journals on primary English.
2. List the key features of the action research process described in this chapter.
3. Describe five top tips for writing effective key questions in primary English, teaching and learning research.
4. List three examples of cross-curricular primary English research themes.

Further Reading

The British Dyslexia Association (http://www.bdadyslexia.org.uk).

Centre for Literacy in Primary Education. (2011) Power of reading project. Electronic version from www.clpe.co.uk

The National Association for Language Development in the Curriculum (http://www.naldic.org.uk).

Mullis, I.V.S., Martin, M.O., Gonzalez, E.J. and Kennedy, A.M. (2007) *Progress in international literacy study [PIRLS]*. Boston MA: International Association for the Evaluation of Education.

Ofsted (2011) *Removing the barriers to literacy*. London: Office for Standards in Education.

OECD (2010) *PISA 2009 Results: What pupils know and can do. Pupil performance in reading, mathematics and science* (Vol. 1). New York: Organisation for Economic Cooperation and Development.

Rose, J. (2006) *Independent review of early reading: Final report*. London: Department for Education and Science.

The United Kingdom Literacy Association (http://www.ukla.org).

References

British Dyslexia Association (BDA) www.bdadyslexia.org.uk

BBC (2011) Learning zone broadband class clips. Retrieved January, 2012, from http://www.bbc.co.uk/learningzone/clips/victorian-school-inspection/155.html

Black, P. and Wiliam, D. (1998) *Inside the black box: Raising standards through classroom assessment*. London: King's College.

Cassidy, J., Montalvo-Valadez, C. and Dee-Gareet, S. (2010) Adolescent and adult literacy: What's hot, what's not, *Journal of Adolescent and Adult Literacy*, 53(6), 444–456.

Chomsky, N. (1965) *Aspects of the theory of syntax*. MIT Press.

Cohen, L., Manion, L. and Morrison, K. (2005) *Research methods in education* (5th edition). London: Routledge Falmer.

Cremin, T., Mottram, M., Bearne, E. and Goodwin, P. (2008) Exploring teacher's knowledge of children's literature. *Cambridge Journal of Education*, 38, 449–464.

Cremin, T., Mottram, M., Powell, F. and Safford, K. (2009) Teachers as readers: Building communities of readers. *Literacy*, 43, 11–19.

Department of Education and Science (DES) (1975) *A Language for Life. The Bullock Report*. London: HMSO.

Dillon, D.R., O'Brien, D. and Heilman, E.E. (2004) Literacy research in the next millennium: From paradigms to pragmatism and practicality. In R. Ruddell and N. Unrau (eds), *Theoretical models and processes of reading* (Vol. 5, pp. 1530–1556). Newark: International Reading Association.

National Literacy Trust (2009) *What's Hot, What's Not.* (Electronic version), *3*. Retrieved 8.8.2011, from www.nationalliteracytrust.org.uk/research

Office for Standards in Education (2011) *Excellence in English: What we can learn from 12 outstanding schools.* No: 100229. London: Office for Standards in Education.

Rose, J. (2006) *Independent review of early reading: Final report.* London: Department for Education and Science.

Stanovich, K.E. (1986) Matthew effects in reading: Some consequences of individual differences in the acquisition of literacy. In R. Ruddell and N. Unrau (eds) *Theoretical models and processes of reading* (Vol. 5, pp. 454–516). Newark: International Reading Association.

Wray, D., Medwell, J., Poulson, L. and Fox, R. (2002) *Teaching Literacy Effectively in the Primary School.* London: Routledge Falmer.

9. Global perspectives

- set homework and plan other out-of-class activities to consolidate and extend the knowledge and understanding pupils have acquired
- contribute to the design and provision of an engaging curriculum within the relevant subject area(s)

5. **Adapt teaching to respond to the strengths and needs of all pupils**
- have a clear understanding of the needs of all pupils, including those with special educational needs; those of high ability; those with English as an additional language; those with disabilities; and be able to use and evaluate distinctive teaching approaches to engage and support them

Introduction

The children you will teach live in an increasingly globalised world. They are immersed in rich diversity and global interdependence of which perhaps they are not aware. It is important that children are taught about the world they live in and encouraged to develop understanding of and thus respect for the wider world and those who inhabit it. You should strive towards the development of global awareness and aim to enable children to become responsible global citizens. English is powerful and effective as a medium to augment children's journeys towards these goals. A broad subject such as the global perspective lends itself easily to cross-curricular links. In fact, as the interconnectedness of the world is examined, opportunities for cross-curricular learning emerge naturally. This chapter explores how children's global awareness and understanding can be developed through English across the curriculum.

What is 'the global perspective'?

In 2005, the DfES introduced guidance entitled *Developing a Global Dimension in the School Curriculum*. Within this guidance, a global dimension incorporates 'key concepts of global citizenship, conflict resolution, diversity, human rights, interdependence, social justice, sustainable development and values and perceptions. It explores the interconnections between the local and the global' (DfES, 2005).

This remains a relevant remit for the subject of the global perspective to be considered in this chapter. The terms 'global dimension' and 'global perspective' are interchangeable in this context. It is through engaging children in learning and discussion about aforementioned key concepts that global citizens are developed. Children can become aware of the wider world and their place within it by engaging in positive exploration of and meaningful dialogue about these concepts.

There is no doubt that children live in a globally interdependent world. They are connected to others and are affected by events and situations far from their immediate environment. Their actions and the choices they make impact upon not only themselves and those around them, but others further afield. Children are increasingly exposed to the wider world, through the media, the internet, travel, food and the multicultural society in which they live. Children may be aware of events in other parts of the world but may have little understanding of the reasons for or consequences of these events. They benefit from becoming aware of the inter-connectedness of human beings around the world. As the wider world becomes more inter-reliant and more accessible, it is crucial that this understanding be developed.

Activity

Consider your day so far. Think about what you have done, what you have used and what you have eaten. Consider the global interdependence of your day so far. How has globalisation and a 'shrinking world' affected your choices today? An example for you to consider follows.

7am: Awoken by alarm clock (made in Japan). An American music hit, popular in many countries around the world, played on my German manufactured digital radio.

7.15am: Showered (consider usage of water in relation to water shortages/lack of access to clean water in other parts of the world), using animal-cruelty free, organic shower gel. Central heating (recent price increase attributed to conflict in oil-producing nations) and lighting (bills for which have recently become problematic as a result of global economic downturn) on in bathroom (Spanish tiled floor, English ceramic sink).

7.30am: Breakfast; oats from Scotland, Fair Trade bananas from Costa Rica (consider the impact of this food choice), organic milk (consider the effect of pesticides on our environment and health), Colombian coffee, bread produced and bought at local farmer's market, honey imported from Ecuador (availability limited after environmental disaster), strawberries from Kenya (consider the air miles), heavily packaged cereal bar (consider the environmental impact) and a croissant, a taste for which was developed during a recent weekend trip to Paris.

8am: Coffee en route to work, purchased at large international conglomerate coffee shop, despite negative publicity concerning unfair deals for coffee farmers, drunk from disposable cup made of paper and plastic. Made phone call, despite the recent community demonstration against the erection of a mobile phone mast near the local primary school, using mobile phone manufactured by Swedish company using minerals mined using child labour and exacerbating conflict in Democratic Republic of Congo.

8.15am: Drove to work in vehicle made in Germany, car pooled with colleagues, using petrol purchased at prices inflated by current global oil crisis......

When you begin to itemise your daily activities in this way, you will notice how dependent we are on the rest of the world and how our choices can have far-reaching consequences. This is an activity worth adapting to undertake with the children in the classes you will teach in order to introduce or highlight the interdependent nature of the global dimension. As DCSF stated 'There is a global dimension to every aspect of life and communities' (2008).

Links to the National Curriculum

The global dimension is apparent in many areas of the primary school curriculum. It can be taught through the existing daily timetable without any additional space being created to incorporate it, but it is prudent to be aware of the potential beyond the prescribed curriculum suggestions. The global perspective is central to the curriculum for geography, as children are developing 'knowledge and understanding of places, patterns and processes', and 'environmental change and sustainable development' and are asking questions 'about people, places and environments' (DfE, 2011a). The global perspective is also pivotal in the non-statutory curriculum for Citizenship at Key Stage 1 and Key Stage 2. Learning about Citizenship requires children to debate topical issues, recognise that the choices they make have consequences and that they have some responsibility towards others and to be aware that they are members of groups and communities (DFE, 2011a). The potential to utilise ICT in learning is rich. Children can, for example, undertake internet research, consult websites, link with other children around the world through social networks or email and can present their learning using ICT. The global perspective features in other curriculum areas for example exploring music from different cultures and learning about significant people and events in Britain and the wider world in history.

Why focus on the global perspective?

Children are protected under international conventions and human rights, affected by events in the world and have some effect on others. Therefore it is imperative that they are guided to consider issues and complexities and to enhance their global awareness and understanding. This involves developing knowledge but also, importantly, attitudes and values. It is not incumbent on you to shape children's thinking, but they should be encouraged to question injustices such as war and poverty and to develop some concept of shared responsibility for their world and the people who inhabit it. Imposing values and beliefs is not advocated, what is suggested is exploration of the global dimension in a way that engages children in discussion and thought about social and moral responsibility. Oxfam Education (2006) argue that it is not enough simply to explore global issues, but that global citizenship is 'about understanding the need to tackle injustice and inequality and having the desire and ability to work actively to do so' (Young and Commins, 2002, p1). Oxfam Education state that valuing and safeguarding the Earth and being aware of their responsibilities towards each other are outcomes of children's learning about global citizenship. Therefore your aim should be for children to be aware of, concerned about and feel some involvement in and responsibility towards the global dimension; their world.

Children have experienced and been variously exposed to a global dimension, but may erroneously perceive it as something 'out there', the 'rest of the world'. They may not yet have positioned themselves within that world or considered their part in it. It is necessary in order to develop global responsibility that children develop an interest in and understanding of connectedness.

In order to create positive change in the world, future generations must be equipped to deal with and respond to global issues and to accept and embrace the interdependence of people. It is hoped that with understanding, children will be able to make choices as informed, responsible, ethical, sensitive global citizens. Enhanced global awareness and cultural sensitivity may enable more harmonious relationships and socially and globally responsible behaviours. Indeed, children's understanding of the changing world and their place within it could ignite a desire and/or a sense of responsibility to care for that world and even to make it a better place. Certainly engaging children in this learning and, crucially, in discourse and analysis of the global perspective has potential for positive and far-reaching consequences.

Many children need and want to be able to understand, at an appropriate level, the reasons for events and circumstances in the world and the impact of these as well as the causes. Through learning about important world concerns, they can examine their own behaviour and make positive contributions to the world. In fact, a recent MORI (Market and Opinion Research International) poll (DEA Ipsos, 2008) suggests that those who have experienced global learning in school are:

- keen to understand more about the problems in the world;
- more likely to believe that what they do in their daily lives can affect those in other countries and that people like them have the ability to make a difference;
- more open to people of different backgrounds;
- more likely to try to do things to make the world a better place.

Ofsted's 2009 report *Education for Sustainable Development* echoed similar positive findings when children were engaged in learning about sustainability. It stated that

'The pupils who were committed to sustainability in school tended to lead sustainable lives at home and there was increasing evidence of this leading to positive changes in their families' views and behaviour. The commitment, enthusiasm and initiative of young people were also a spur to members of the wider community to re-examine their own lifestyles.' (Ofsted, 2009)

Furthermore, recent research from Think Global and YouGov suggests that parents also want their children to be educated about global issues. This 'presents compelling arguments to ensure our schools prepare young people to live, work and contribute in a globalised world' (Think Global, 2011).

Considerations when exploring the global perspective

It is essential that, although serious and perhaps distressing, uncomfortable and difficult situations are explored, children feel safe, secure and supported in coping with such issues. Care must be taken to render the content of the learning age and stage appropriate and not to create fear or anxiety, or a negative world view, in children. This can be achieved partly through open, honest and scaffolded discussion facilitated with sensitivity and perceptiveness. It will be necessary to select and edit or adapt what is explored very carefully. Resources are produced that can assist you in ensuring appropriateness and these will be discussed under the 'Further Reading' heading of this chapter.

Sensitivity and secure subject knowledge are required on your part when delving into global concerns such as poverty, inequality and conflict in order not to perpetuate negative stereotypes. All too often, children are bombarded with damaging representations and an overtone of difference; it is possible that children develop a perspective of 'them and us'. Although issues can and should be explored, it is a requisite that children be taught that these are not confined to certain places in the world, neither do they define those places. In fact, a celebratory approach should be taken to exploring the world; one that focuses on, for example, similarity rather than difference. Care should be taken to ensure positive representations and break stereotypes and preconceived negative ideas. For children to develop as global citizens, it is helpful to concentrate on what they have in common with others, rather than how they may differ. They should learn to celebrate diversity and to respect difference, but to also notice common ground or shared interests. Children should learn about others and also from others.

The following case study is one example of exploring the global dimension in a positive way, focusing on one country and attempting to avoid a limited or one-dimensional view of this country and its people.

Case Study: Children learning about Ethiopia

Alison is a trainee teacher working alongside an experienced teacher in a class of upper Key Stage 2 children. The children have been learning about Ethiopia as part of their class topic. So far, this has focused mainly on geography and the children have been fascinated to learn about the varied landscapes and climates within the country. They have begun to understand why drought and famine have occurred and to explore the factors which can exacerbate such disasters. Alison is concerned that the children are developing a negative overview as their learning has centred predominantly on the difficulties some people may experience in Ethiopia. Although she accepts that valuable learning is occurring and that what the children are discovering is factually accurate, she discusses with the class teacher the possibility of broadening the learning to present a more comprehensive picture of the country and its people.

→

Alison uses the internet to select and show videos of different forms of Ethiopian dance and uses these as the core of several PE lessons. She is able to invite members of the local Ethiopian community to teach the children some dancing, which proves very popular and enjoyable.

Alison explores with the children the rich and fascinating culture through music, dance, food, legends and history. She takes the opportunity to develop mathematics learning through investigation of the Ethiopian calendar and the system used for telling the time. She also reads and shares some stories. Alison focuses on the leisure activities of Ethiopians, hoping to demonstrate everyday life rather than disasters and to suggest interests and desires not dissimilar to the children's. By focusing on the people, Alison makes the learning more about people and helps the children to consider what life in Ethiopia might be like, being careful also not to suggest homogeneity. She consistently draws out lifestyle similarities through discussion of celebrations, family, hobbies and so on. She also mentions the popularity of English Premier League football amongst the population in Ethiopia.

Alison extends the learning to focus on coffee, an important Ethiopian export and a very important part of the culture. She explores the legend which situates Ethiopia as the birthplace of coffee. Cross-curricular links are made to history as children explore legend as well as the history of coffee and its consumption. From this, the children are able to learn about the farming and manufacture of coffee. This links with geography as climate, landscape and land use are considered. They learn something about the export of coffee and its popularity around the world and investigate its place in different cultures, including their own. This leads to further learning about fair trade and responsible shopping, with both geography and PSHE foci.

The children are interested and engaged and undertake much independent research. Alison decides that learning could be extended and deepened by establishing contact with children in Ethiopia and seeks to set up pen pal links.

Links to the National Curriculum

A wealth of learning occurs in the above case study and links to the curriculum are plentiful. Firstly, in English, the children have been developing reading skills in reading to find information, learning about different text types whilst studying legends and simultaneously broadening their experience of stories from different cultures. When writing to pen pals, the children will develop skills in choosing form and content to suit a particular context and using language and style that are appropriate for the reader. Geography is also key to the learning as children 'begin to recognise and describe geographical patterns and to appreciate the importance of wider geographical location in understanding places. They recognise and describe physical and human processes. They begin to understand how these can change the features of places, and how these changes affect the lives and activities of people living there' (DfE, 2011b). Mathematical learning is rich as the numerous problem solving tasks are presented. Other curriculum links include PE, as the children 'create and perform dances using a range of movement patterns, including those from different times, places and cultures' (DfE, 2011b).

International school links

The idea of establishing and maintaining contact between children in your class and children in another part of the world is an excellent one. This enables constructive personal contact and the potential to explore another country and culture through a one-to-one relationship with someone from that country. It is possible to break down barriers and shatter stereotypes through such individual liaison. Such connections can be extremely valuable and positive for all parties involved as extensive learning can occur through communication and the forging of friendships.

However, constraints exist and care should be taken to enter into such connections responsibly and wisely. Rather than perpetuate negative stereotypes, the mutual benefits should be emphasised. The intention is that children in different parts of the world form relationships and learn about and from each other, it is not a fund-raising activity nor a one-sided fact finding mission. Intentions and aims should be discussed and agreed by all those with responsibility for the communication. It is also important that the pen-pal relationship can be maintained and is not entirely dependent on particular individuals; you as a trainee teacher who will soon leave the school, for example. Additionally, implications and limitations should be considered carefully. For example, there may be financial constraints on the regular sending of mail if this method is selected, or limited or unreliable availability of the internet if email is the chosen medium. Careful research, sensitivity and open communication about the purpose, process and longevity of the pen-pal relationship are required. The following case study outlines one trainee teacher's experiences.

Case Study: Exploring international school links

Maddie is a trainee teacher working with a Year 3 class. She has been asked to set up a link with a school in Southern India and so undertakes research to assess the possibility.

She begins by researching online, finding http://schoolsonline.britishcouncil.org/home to be particularly helpful. She then speaks to colleagues who have had some experience of international school links.

$\rightarrow$

Maddie's initial findings suggest that establishing this independently may prove ineffective in the long-term. She speaks to several teachers and head teachers who report that they had such links in the past, but no longer do.

Maddie discovers that this is usually because the person at the school who was responsible for setting up the link has either left the school or been unable to continue the project. She also speaks to one teacher whose class were very excited about their newly established international school link only to become frustrated at the delay in receiving replies through the post. Another teacher reported that her school link had been discontinued when the overseas school lost its internet connection.

Maddie concludes that the international school links that remained successful for all parties involved appeared to be those established with longevity in mind and clarity pertaining to expectations, procedures and logistics. These links were characterised by mutual understanding and common shared goals. Many successful introductions had been facilitated through Global School Partnerships. Maddie discovers that

> The Global School Partnerships programme is funded by the Department for International Development (DFID) with the aim of motivating young people's commitment to a fairer, more sustainable world. DFID supports school partnerships that promote global education through the curriculum. Support and guidance is provided to teachers and grants to schools to make the most of a school partnership as a learning tool. Funding is available for visits between partner schools to enable them to develop curriculum projects together based on global themes.
>
> Global School Partnerships programme: Impact evaluation
> (Sizmur et al., 2011)

Maddie reads the information about how to set up a partnership and is inspired by some of the case studies. She contacts GSP through the website www.dfid.gov.uk/get-involved/in-your-school/global-school-partnerships and has soon established a link. The project has open-ended cross-curricular potential as not only is children's writing a focus, but the long-term partnership could result in numerous projects and curriculum areas being exploited. Maddie decides to begin with introductory letters from the children in both classes as well as the teachers, to see where this might lead the children's interests.

....

Research Focus

There has long been interest in teaching children about the global perspective and this has taken different forms throughout educational history. What was once considered 'education for international understanding' early in the twentieth century became known as 'world studies' in the 1950s and 1960s, when the focus shifted slightly to emphasise the need for a world-centred perspective in education.

From the 1970s until the present day, NGOs (non-governmental organisations) included in their development work the targeting of schools to help to tackle global inequality and bring about change. This tends to concentrate on attitudinal change through awareness-raising and the promotion of children's knowledge and understanding of global issues. Specifically produced teaching materials and resources support teachers to facilitate effective and appropriate learning about global issues. Alongside this, NGOs aim also to develop teachers' knowledge and expertise, through training and materials. Large charities such as Unicef and Oxfam have been particularly active and influential in education in recent years.

Since the early 1990s, The Development Education Association (DEA) has coordinated development education in the UK and is responsible for Development Education Centres (DECs) across the country. Focal points of education, in their view, are exploring links, understanding reasons for inequity and working towards eradicating this and making the world a fairer place.

An educative outline of the history of teaching the global dimension in schools can be found in Hicks and Holden's 2007 text *Teaching the Global Dimension: key principles and effective practice*.

As previously mentioned, in 2005 the DfES published *Developing a Global Dimension in the School Curriculum*. This guidance emphasised the placing of the curriculum within a broad, global context. It also demonstrated how all curriculum subjects could incorporate the global dimension. This was supported by the 2008 DCSF publication *Top Tips to Develop the Global Dimension in Schools*, which utilised successful, effective examples to provide further advice. At the time of writing, more current government guidance on teaching the global dimension in primary schools is awaited.

The curriculum review commissioned by the previous government placed considerable emphasis on the global dimension. In the Cambridge Primary Review, Professor Robin Alexander stated the importance of teaching which highlights 'The individual in relation to others and the wider world: encouraging

$\rightarrow$

respect and reciprocity; promoting interdependence and sustainability; empowering local, national and global citizenship; celebrating culture and community' (Alexander, 2009).

The curriculum guidance published in 2009 listed the global dimension as one of the seven cross-curriculum dimensions and is introduced by Mick Waters, the then Director of Curriculum at QCA, by this statement; 'We want young people to understand, consider and influence the world in which they live. The curriculum has to help them to explore key dimensions by bringing their learning together around key issues that affect our changing society' (Alexander, 2009, p2).

As this book goes to publication, it is assumed that, although a change in government has rendered this particular curriculum guidance obsolete, a similar acknowledgement of the importance of the global dimension in the curriculum is likely to be present in the 2014 curriculum. An article published on the Department for Education website in November 2011 presented the non-statutory guidance on Citizenship alongside cross-curriculum references, which suggested an approach in line with that of this book. Indeed in the foreword to *Teaching the Global Dimension* Mick Waters writes:

> *A curriculum fit for purpose in the twenty-first century should encourage the development of critically thinking pupils who are not only aware of global issues and events ... but also realise that they can be effective participators in working on challenges, solutions and opportunities (Hicks and Holden, 2007, xi). In fact, the DfE Expert Panel Review's recommendation at this stage is that 'Citizenship is of enormous importance in a contemporary and future-oriented education. However, we are not persuaded that study of the issues and topics included in citizenship education constitutes a distinct 'subject' as such. We therefore recommend that it be reclassified as part of the Basic Curriculum.*

> *(DfE, 2011a)*

Key texts in the study of global education in primary schools include the 2002 Oxfam publication *Global Citizenship, the Handbook for Primary Teaching* by Young and Commins. The ideas presented here are an excellent starting point for teachers who strive to teach key concepts confidently.

An eminent academic in the field of global education is David Hicks. His 2007 text, co-edited with Cathie Holden, *Teaching the Global Dimension* contains key ideas and theory. Hicks' emphasis is on children's interdependence and connectedness. He asserts 'Exploration of *local-global* connections is at the heart of global education, since these dimensions are inextricably related and relevant to all subject areas.' (Hicks, 2012)

$\rightarrow$

Miriam Steiner's 1996 work *Developing the Global Teacher* is also of value: here she recognises the formation of a global society and investigates the meanings of global citizenship. She draws on and is in support of James Lynch's work, particularly his argument of the vital role schools play in providing education for 'active global democracy' as outlined in the 1992 volume of *Human Rights, Education, & Global Responsibilities*. (Lynch et al.)

One significant initiative in the promotion of global school links has been the work of Global Schools Partnerships, funded by DFID and supported by the British Council. The emphasis on reciprocal learning and equity of relationships is crucial. Edification is enabled through the establishment and maintenance of communicative links between a school in the UK and one in another part of the world, with relationships between children and staff based on mutual respect and learning. Recent analysis of such partnerships can be found in the Global School Partnership Programme Evaluation Report available at www.nfer.ac.uk/publiations.GSPP POI.pdf. The report concludes that

> The Global School Partnerships programme aims to motivate young people's commitment to a fairer, more sustainable world. The evidence from this research indicates that the GSP programme has made a significant positive impact on the learning and attitudes of girls and boys in primary and secondary schools throughout the UK.

> *(2011)*

Global education, thus the global perspective as defined by this chapter, remains an important and much debated aspect of primary school teaching. Research continues to be undertaken to elucidate why it should and how it can be effectively addressed. The current emphasis is, in the words of Hicks and Holden '... on both changing self and changing society for neither is possible without the other' (2007).

Using texts to explore the global dimension

As discussed in Chapter 3, children's literature is an excellent vehicle for learning and can certainly be utilised to teach about the global dimension. Chapter 4 explored the possibility of using non-fiction texts in a cross-curricular manner and this would be an appropriate and excellent approach to teaching about the global dimension. Searching the internet, speaking to colleagues and asking at your local library should provide ideas as to the wealth of texts available to teach this broad topic. In addition, many NGOs and charities produce excellent educational material. You may want to share specifically produced texts which explore different aspects of the global dimension, or you may wish to focus on books from a particular country or area of the world. There are endless possibilities and using texts has the added advantage of bringing the subject matter alive in a non-threatening, appropriate and exciting way. The following two case studies provide examples of this.

Case Study: Outlining the use of a book to stimulate learning about the global perspective

Trainee teacher Rosie has selected the book *If the World Were One Village* by David J Smith and Shelagh Armstrong as a starting point for a topic and plans to generate learning across the curriculum through its use.

She first reads the book to the Year 6 class and facilitates open-ended and personal responses from the children. Rosie wants the children to lead the learning and has been very flexible in her planning, willing to plan the learning according to the children's responses and interests.

First, the children are interested in the mathematics and Rosie designs several investigations based on the facts and figures presented within the book, particularly information about populations. The children present the information in different formats, including pie charts and graphs. She also asks them to enquire into how these figures were arrived at and what statistical evaluation would have been done, based on which figures. They do this using a range of sources, including the internet and reference texts. The children design surveys which would access the kinds of information in the book and discuss statistic collection such as censuses and the reasons for undertaking these. They examine the purpose and use of such statistics and also the impediments to guaranteeing accuracy.

Next the children want to explore some of the places in the world that are mentioned in the book and Rosie prepares some geography focused work which will develop their understanding of maps and of environments. The children select different locations and then undertake thorough research, using texts, maps and the internet, to find out as much as they can about the country, its people, landscape and so on. This becomes a long-term project with children working in pairs on their chosen locations and producing leaflets about them using their ICT skills. The children also want to explore nationalities and different languages. They are able to establish links and to learn a few words in some of the languages.

They also explore the faiths mentioned and produce fact files for each one, based on their research and visits to places of worship.

The children are fascinated by the information about access to water and electricity and begin to investigate why not everyone has this. This encompasses learning about governance, poverty, sustainability, waste and conflict. The children are inspired to take this learning further and begin to focus the next class topic on issues of equality and global citizenship.

Links to the National Curriculum

The children in Rosie's class led the learning and in this way natural cross-curricular links were made. However, Rosie was diligent and careful to ensure that the statutory requirements of the NC were also addressed.

The research undertaken by the children linked to English, but also directly to that for ICT. They talked about the information they needed and where to find and use it and interpreted this carefully.

They also undertook mathematics investigations and thoroughly explored, interrogated and drew conclusions about data.

The NC links for geography were extensive. Geographical enquiry and skills were developed as the children asked questions, collected and recorded evidence, analysed this and drew conclusions from it and communicated their findings appropriately and effectively. They went on to use appropriate geographical vocabulary and to use atlases, globes and maps and secondary sources of information . Their geographical investigations used ICT and involved decision-making skills. By the end of the research projects, children were able to describe what places are like and their locations and to explain why they are as they are and how they have changed and may change in the future. The interdependence of people and places was a key learning point. The children's interest in sustainable development became an inspiring project for them. They became very conscious of countries which are less economically developed and this led onto some inspiring PSHE and citizenship related learning.

The children thought carefully about people in different places, the allocation of resources and the effects of governance and democracy. They also developed knowledge about RE and have a greater understanding of some faith groups.

The preceding and following case studies illustrate the potential of using a book as a starting point to stimulate cross-curricular learning which explores the global dimension. These books were particularly suited to this purpose and were selected by the trainee teachers to be appropriate for the children and the learning. You will discover a wealth of texts which can be used similarly. The suggestions in Chapter 3 will help you to familiarise yourself with the wonderful range of books available.

Case Study: Exploring Britain

Trainee teacher Brian is working in a Year 4 class who have been working on Britain since the 1930s in their history topic. He decides to explore Britain with the class and asks the children to discuss the country in its entirety. This proves challenging and Brian realises that there are very different perceptions, sometimes based on

→

children's individual backgrounds, the places they have travelled to and what they may have seen on television. Brian is fascinated by the range of experiences and viewpoints in the class. He brings in many travel brochures and the children look online at information about different countries. From this, they are asked to create in groups a travel brochure for Britain. They are asked to include highlights, information about the people, food, cultures, sightseeing, climate, transport, pastimes and anything else they think relevant or important. The work the children produce is varied and from this Brian generates some interesting discussion about national identity (at a very basic level). He realises that perhaps Britain is too broad and the children's experiences are insufficient to produce factual information about the country as a whole. He decides to focus in on the local area and the very immediate environment and adapt the learning to concentrate more locally.

To conclude, Brian uses the picture book *ABC UK* by James Dunn and Helen Bate to explore the variety and vibrancy of Britain. He asks the children to create a similar book; the ABC of their local environment. The discussion after sharing *ABC UK* with the children inspires Brian to take each page as a starting point for the children's learning. For example, the children want to know why 'J is for Jury' and find out about the legal system and its origins. Similarly, 'V is for Vindaloo' initiates much lively and enlightening discussion about food.

Brian realises that each child is immersed in a multitude of cultures, none of which can or should be neatly defined and that the diversity of Britain is an exploration offering open-ended learning opportunities and endless possibilities.

Approaches to teaching the global dimension

The previous case studies demonstrate different examples of the global dimension being explored with children. An alternative approach could be a topic based approach, where a theme is selected, preferably with input from the children to ensure child-led learning and to take into consideration their interests and experiences. The selected theme may form the framework for the learning, with cross-curricular opportunities being planned around it. For example, you might choose to explore a broad topic such as music. This would enable opportunities for positive and fascinating learning about music around the world, where different instruments originate, how music has developed, popularity of musical genres, famous musicians, traditional styles of music, fusions of different styles of music, music for special occasions and so on.

You could instead decide to focus on languages, looking at the import and export of words from different languages, how English has evolved and continues to do so, (as outlined in Chapter 2) which languages are spoken by children in your class,(as suggested in Chapter 5) migration, disappearing languages and so on. Other topics might include world leaders, influential people, inventions, travel, migration, sport, clothes, fashion, manufacturing...

Case Study: Illustrating planning learning around a topic

Jenny is going to plan the learning of her Year 4 placement class around a topic from a selection suggested by the children. She intends to plan to ensure curriculum coverage and the development of key skills and knowledge, but takes a flexible approach as she hopes the children will lead the learning, taking it in directions based on their interests and what they want to find out.

Jenny chooses the topic of 'food' as the starting point. She first asks the class to thought shower and jot down all they know and all they want to know (using a KWL grid as discussed in Chapter 4) about food, first individually, then in small groups and eventually as a whole class. From this, Jenny is able to select key themes to begin planning the learning.

Jenny introduces the topic by presenting to the children a pizza with various toppings. She asks the children where the pizza has come from which initiates discussion of local retailers, food delivery options and restaurants. Jenny unpicks the question further and the children begin to research more thoroughly, finding out where different ingredients come from. They are amazed to discover the international flavour of the pizza which comprises ingredients from all over the world. A great deal of geography learning occurs through Internet research and map reading as well as finding out why certain goods are grown or produced in certain countries. Jenny uses the opportunity to develop mathematics skills by exploring food miles. She also introduces the concepts of fair trade and buying locally produced goods.

Jenny explores with the children the food they eat and the origins of both the ingredients and the dish itself. The children keep food diaries and are fascinated to learn how international their daily diet is. Reasons for this are explored and themes such as immigration and travel are sensitively and simply discussed.

Jenny is able to invite parents and children to share different foods. The children are able to taste and also to prepare some different foods and later attempt to create and use different recipes. This culminates in an international food evening to which parents and other members of the community are invited.

The children want to know more about special foods and those connected to religious or significant events and this forms the next part of the topic.

The previous case study highlights the wonderfully rich and diverse society of which the children are part. By exploring food, the children begin to recognise the many nationalities and cultures present in this country and the myriad of influences on their daily diet. Children could question what are considered 'traditional' food or local delicacies. This could form the beginnings of constructive exploration of their own identities and cultures whilst demonstrating global interdependence.

Learning Outcomes Review

This chapter has described the importance of maximising opportunities to incorporate the global dimension in your teaching. It has discussed some ways in which this can be achieved. The case studies have detailed varied examples of the global dimension being explored with primary school children in a cross-curricular manner.

Self-assessment questions

1. Why is it important that children's learning takes account of the global perspective?
2. Can you suggest ways to use English, in a cross-curricular way, to develop children's global awareness?
3. How can English contribute to the development of children as global citizens?
4. Suggest three examples of learning which incorporate the global perspective in a cross-curricular way.
5. Suggest three ways in which English can be used to explore aspects of the world in which children live.
6. Can you think of any other examples of using English to explore the global perspective, in addition to the ones described in this chapter?

Further Reading

The Research Focus section of this chapter provides some suggestions as to further reading for you to develop your knowledge and understanding of teaching the global perspective.

Hicks, D. and Holden, C. (2007) *Teaching the Global Dimension: key principles and effective practice*. London: Routledge.
This is recommended reading not least for an overview of the historical perspective of how the global dimension has been addressed in schools.

Young, M. and Commins, E. (2002) *Global Citizenship: The Handbook for Primary Teaching*. Oxfam, Chris Kington Publishing.
This is an excellent starting point for trainee teachers to become familiar with how to successfully implement this aspect of education.

In the absence of more recent government guidelines, the 2005 DFES publication *Developing a Global Dimension in the School Curriculum* and the more recent (2008) DCSF guidance *Top Tips to Develop the Global Dimension in Schools* are excellent sources of information and ideas.

Beyond that, it is advised that your further reading comprise a thorough exploration of the resources and materials available for teachers to develop the global perspective in their classrooms. This should include investigating the DEA and any DECs (Development Education Centres) local to you, or accessible online.

In addition, the websites of most NGOs include a section entitled 'education', 'teachers' or 'schools' and often provide high quality, relevant and inspiring resources, activities and information. Listed below (in alphabetical order) are some that the authors have found particularly valuable, but it is expedient for you to spend some time finding the resources and websites that are most relevant and appropriate for the teaching you would like to undertake.

www.christianaid.org.uk (includes some fabulous games and activities produced by this NGO, for example the 'paper bag game').

www.fairtrade.org.uk/schools/ (ideas for teaching about fair trade).

www.globaldimension.org.uk (great range of activities and resources).

www.oxfam.org.uk (information about global issues).

www.oxfam.org.uk/coolplanet/kidsweb (aimed at children, an excellent, age-appropriate and highly engaging website full of excellent information and activities for children).

http://www.risc.org.uk/education (offers a database of over 9,000 books and teaching materials).

www.savethechildren.org.uk/teachers (excellent ideas and resources).

www.think-global.org.uk (a charity working to educate and engage people about global issues, some excellent resources available and lots of information about current issues and research).

www.tidec.org/primary-early-years (global learning bank of resources and teaching ideas).

www.unicef.org.uk/Education (teaching resources and excellent initiatives such as the Rights Respecting Schools Awards).

References

Alexander, R. (2009) *Children, their World, their Education: final report and recommendations of the Cambridge Primary Review.* London: Routledge.

DCSF (2008) *Top Tips to Develop the Global Dimension in Schools DCSF*-00683-2008.

Development Education Assciation (DEA) IPSOS (2008) *Young People's Experiences of Global Learning: An Ipsos MORI Research Study on behalf of DEA.* Available at: www.think-global.org.uk/research

DfE (2011a) The Framework for the National Curriculum – A report by the Expert Panel for the National Curriculum review, DFE-00135-2011.

DfE (2011b) www.education.gov.uk/schools/teachingandlearning/curriculum/primary/b00199167/pe/ks2

DfES (2005) *Developing a Global Dimension in the School Curriculum* Reference:DFES-1409-2005. Available as archive material at https://www.education.gov.uk/publications/standard/publicationdetail/page1/DFES-1409-2005

Hicks, D. (2012) *Teaching for a Better World* available online at http://www.teaching4abetterworld.co.uk/global.html

Hicks, D. and Holden, C. (2007) *Teaching the Global Dimension: key principles and effective practice.* London: Routledge.

Invernizzi A. and Williams J. (eds) (2007) *Children and Citizenship.* London: SAGE.

Lynch, J., Modgil, C. and Modgil, S. (1992) *Human Rights, Education, & Global Responsibilities, Volume 3.* UK: RoutledgeFalmer.

Ofsted (2009) *Education for Sustainable Development.* Available at: www.ofsted.gov.uk/Ofsted-home/Publications-and-research/Browse-all- by/Documents-by-type/Thematic-reports/Education-for-sustainable-development-improving-schools-improving-lives

Oxfam Development Education Programme (2006) *Education for Global Citizenship a Guide for Schools.* Oxfam: available at www.oxfam.org.uk

Sizmur, J., Brzyska, B., Cooper, L., Morrison, J., Wilkinson, K. and Kerr, D. (2011) *Global School Partnerships programme: Impact evaluation report.* London: DFID. Available from http://www.nfer.ac.uk/nfer/publications/GSPP01/01_home.cfm?publicationID=582&title=Global%20School%20Partnerships%20programme:%20Impact%20evaluation.

Stenier, M. (ed) (1996) *Developing the Global Teacher: theory and practice in initial teacher education.* Stoke on Trent: Trentham Books.

Think Global (2011) *What parents want: the role of schools in teaching about the wider world: a briefing for policy makers.* Available from http://think-global.org.uk/resources/item.asp?d=4480 Think Global, 2011.

Think Global (2012) Available at: www.think-global.org.uk/index.asp

QCA (2009) *Cross-curriculum Dimensions: A Planning Guide for Schools*, London: Qualifications and Curriculum Authority. Available at http://schoolsonline.britishcouncil.org/sites/default/files/el/98010.pdf

Young, M. and Commins, E. (2002) *Global Citizenship: The Handbook for Primary Teaching.* Oxfam, Chris Kington Publishing.

10. Beyond your initial training: celebrating and promoting English

Learning Outcomes

This chapter aims to help you to:

- reflect on the potential to use and learn about English beyond the context of the school curriculum;
- consider how to organise and manage your own classroom to support children's development in English across the curriculum;
- begin to consider what might be needed for the establishment of a positive classroom ethos for speaking, listening, reading and writing;
- enhance your awareness of how children's pleasure and success in reading impacts on their success across the whole curriculum;
- develop your awareness of the whole school community in relation to English and across the curriculum;
- begin to consider how you might contribute to whole school English activities.

TEACHERS' STANDARDS

A teacher must:

1. Set high expectations which inspire, motivate and challenge pupils

- establish a safe and stimulating environment for pupils, rooted in mutual respect
- demonstrate consistently the positive attitudes, values and behaviour which are expected of pupils

2. Promote good progress and outcomes by pupils

- encourage pupils to take a responsible and conscientious attitude to their own work and study

3. Demonstrate good subject and curriculum knowledge

- have a secure knowledge of the relevant subject(s) and curriculum areas, foster and maintain pupils' interest in the subject, and address misunderstandings
- demonstrate a critical understanding of developments in the subject and curriculum areas, and promote the value of scholarship

4. Plan and teach well structured lessons

- promote a love of learning and children's intellectual curiosity
- set homework and plan other out-of-class activities to consolidate and extend the knowledge and understanding pupils have acquired

- contribute to the design and provision of an engaging curriculum within the relevant subject area(s)

5. **Adapt teaching to respond to the strengths and needs of all pupils**
- have a clear understanding of the needs of all pupils, including those with special educational needs; those of high ability; those with English as an additional language; those with disabilities; and be able to use and evaluate distinctive teaching approaches to engage and support them

6. **Manage behaviour effectively to ensure a good and safe learning environment**
- manage classes effectively, using approaches which are appropriate to pupils' needs in order to involve and motivate them

7. **Fulfil wider professional responsibilities**
- make a positive contribution to the wider life and ethos of the school

Introduction

This book has introduced you to English across the curriculum through consideration of some of the many ways that cross-curricular contexts can provide a meaningful framework for children to consolidate their capability in English and also by exploring how lessons in other subjects can be enhanced through a focus on different aspects of English. Another way to explore English across the curriculum is to reflect on how English is used and celebrated throughout the school day, both within and beyond the classroom. English is much more than a lesson on the timetable: it is the medium through which children access the curriculum and through which all the learning and day-to-day activities of school life will be communicated. English plays a central role in all the work of the classroom and in the community of the school. This chapter reflects on the wider significance of English beyond the specific context of curriculum subjects. It explores classroom routines, ongoing English work and the establishment of a positive classroom ethos for language, literature and literacy particularly in relation to your own classroom as you reach the final stages of your initial teacher training and your NQT year. The ethos of the whole school, and the part that you can play in this, is also considered.

Your own first classroom

You will have taught many literacy lessons during your school placements and may also have had opportunity to plan for English in cross-curricular contexts. This will have given you experience of lesson and medium term planning both within English lessons and across the curriculum. It is very likely, however, that you will have worked within the classroom routines already established by your mentor, without an opportunity to plan for these independently. These routines might include those specific to English such as the organisation and management of a home-school reading scheme and systems for the practice and monitoring of spelling and handwriting. Routines for children's learning across the curriculum and for activities beyond the curriculum also provide really valuable opportunities for developing English competency in a range of meaningful contexts. For example: opportunities to exploit English will occur in communication of the daily and weekly timetable, in the displays and resources you establish for English and other subjects, in the organisation of classroom jobs and 'monitors' and even in how you plan for children's use of the cloakroom. When you become an NQT, it will be your responsibility to establish these routines from the outset. This is likely to be both exciting and slightly daunting and good preparation will be essential to ensure you create a well-organised and rich learning environment within and beyond the curriculum.

Activity

In preparation for the beginning of your first term as a class teacher your immediate task will be one of research. You will need to find out about the school policies that govern everyday routines in English and other subjects and about the routines and policies for aspects of everyday school life.

Some useful questions to ask:	Notes
Is there a set timetable that will need to be communicated to children? How much time, if any, is left for you to allocate to different curriculum subjects?	
Does the school have a homework policy that correlates to the class you will be teaching? What is the expectation?	
Is there a home-school reading policy in operation? How many books do children take home? Do children have a 'book-bag' with a contact diary to record reading opportunities? What is the expectation on the teacher and on parents and guardians in relation to the contact diary? How often are books changed?	
Do children take home spellings or times tables to learn?	
Does the school teaching and learning policy encourage children's independent access to resources?	
Will the children in your class have access to a cloakroom for their coats and bags?	
Where are items such as packed lunches and PE kit stored?	
Drawing on your observation of routines in your school experience placement classrooms what other questions might you want to ask?	

In addition to finding out about school policy and practice you will need to assess the space, furniture and resources in your classroom.

Once you have gathered the information above you will be ready to begin the exciting task of planning the layout of your first classroom. Your initial consideration will probably be the children's requirements which are likely to include a carpeted area, tables and chairs, personal storage facilities such as trays, a space to store finished and unfinished work, a book corner or reading area and, depending on the age of the class, a role play area. As you develop your plans, consider how the environment you are establishing will support children to use English across the school day and across the curriculum. You will want to provide plenty of labeling to signal classroom routines, instructions and responsibilities. Even something very simple such as children's names on trays or coat pegs can provide incidental opportunities for very young children to develop their literacy knowledge. For example adjacent name labels will enable children to notice what the names Mark and Mary have in common and what is different. You may also want to label curriculum resources for children's independent access which will provide a real context for children to read English as they go about their learning. Similarly, the displays you create for all curriculum subjects will provide a further opportunity to use English across the curriculum. You may also have labels and greetings in other languages, recognising and celebrating the linguistic diversity of the school.

You will also need to consider your requirements as the class teacher. If you are going to be a well organised and efficient teacher, and a positive role model for the children, you will need some personal space to store your own resources and records, some of which might be confidential. A more public space, such as a noticeboard, will be very useful for you and will also serve to illustrate to children how English is used to help us organise our daily lives.

Case Study: Setting up your own first classroom to promote and celebrate English across the curriculum

Ruth has just accepted her first teaching post in a Reception class and has been given access to the classroom to begin her preparation for the new school year. She has gathered the necessary information on school policies and practices and is keen to ensure that these are reflected in her classroom layout. Ruth knows that through thoughtful classroom organisation she can encourage children's use of language across the curriculum to support their achievement in the early learning goals.

Ruth decides that initially the role play area will be a traditional 'home corner' offering a familiar context for the children during their first half term at school. The home corner includes everyday objects such as cooking equipment and food packets from a range of cultures. Ruth includes a clock and a set of weighing scales, with which many children will be familiar, to promote mathematical discussion. In addition to the many role play and speaking and listening opportunities the objects will generate, Ruth ensures there is a telephone with a message pad and pencil and other examples of the written word such as memos, an address book, diaries, a calendar, recipe books, a television guide and letters and postcards that have arrived in the post. The written word is everywhere. Later in the year Ruth plans to transform the role play area into different contexts that

$\rightarrow$

will exploit other areas of learning and the use of spoken and written English across the curriculum. Her planned themes include a café, a veterinary surgery, a garden centre, a post office, a library and a supermarket.

Ruth ensures that resources in the classroom are labeled clearly so that children can begin to develop independence in their selection of materials when designing and making. Classroom displays include a number staircase to illustrate ordinal numbers and object pictures with accompanying cardinal numbers to provide examples of quantity. Ruth also displays pictures with examples of mathematical language such as 'more', 'less', 'same', 'smaller', 'bigger', 'heavier' and 'lighter'. A display of shapes incorporated into pictures from a variety of cultures provides a further opportunity for children to engage in discussion using mathematical language. These include circles in a bicycle picture and squares in a picture of a house. Ruth also collects objects made from different materials to support children to use language to explore similarities, differences and patterns.

Ruth has completed an audit of the classroom book corner and has organised the books into labeled boxes and baskets. She also has a collection of story sacks. The book boxes include 'Poetry and Rhymes', 'Information Books' and one called 'Favourite Characters' which includes books featuring characters such as *The Very Hungry Caterpillar*, *Elmer*, *Alfie*, *Spot* and *Kipper*. Ruth has also set up a box called 'Our Favourite Books' into which she plans to put copies of the books she reads aloud to the class.

Links to the National Curriculum

The revised guidance for the Early Years Foundation Stage 2012 specifies three prime areas: personal, social and emotional development, communication and language and physical development. It also identifies four areas of learning: literacy, mathematics, expressive arts and design and understanding the world. Ruth's classroom organisation will support children's development in these areas through:

- a role play area resourced with materials that reflect a range of cultures including children's family lives and communities;
- collections for children to explore, sort, order and label in their play;
- display of numerals and shapes in meaningful contexts and examples of mathematical vocabulary;
- picture books, books with flaps or hidden words, books with accompanying CDs and story sacks;
- materials and opportunities for children to use writing in their play.

First days

Displays across the curriculum are likely to be an important part of your planning and preparation when you take up your first teaching post. You will want to consider a few displays that can be achieved very easily in your first few days as a class teacher. These can help the children, and you, to feel at home in the classroom and will be your first examples of using and promoting English across and beyond the curriculum. Children can be asked to develop a short piece of written work setting out personal strengths or favourite subjects. For very young children this might take the form of a drawing with a simple label. A simple activity such as this helps you to begin to get to know something about the children both through what they choose to tell you about themselves and through being able to make some initial assessments of their work. A display heading such as 'I am good at . . .' offers a very positive beginning for your classroom environment and supports personal, social and health education. Photographs of the children can also be included in the display.

If you are meeting your class in July you may be able to develop some work from your first meeting and have it displayed ready for the start of the new term. Other ideas for quick displays include: months of the year with children's names or photos shown on cakes or balloons for the month of their birthday; a 'Who is here today?' display with photographs or name labels to be added by the children when they arrive in the mornings; a 'How am I feeling board?' where children can add their name to headings such as 'happy, excited', 'ready to learn'; a 'Person of the Week' poster with space for children's photographs and some information about their achievements.

You might also want to think about some 'semi-permanent' classroom displays that will enhance the children's learning across the curriculum throughout the year. Semi-permanent displays can help to facilitate good time management because they are easy to update. These could include a 'word wall' of, for example: adjectives, prefixes and suffixes or connectives and vocabulary banks for other curriculum subjects. An established display board can be revised quickly to link to the current focus.

A particularly important area of the classroom is the book corner or reading area. A stimulating book corner will promote reading and discussion about books and many fiction and non-fiction books will support children to bring additional meaning to their learning across the curriculum.

Case Study: Setting up the classroom book corner

Charlotte is about to start her first teaching post. She has just graduated from a BA QTS degree and is keen to put into practice all she has learned. In particular, Charlotte enjoyed an assignment set during the second year of her programme in which she had to keep a photographic and written record of the development of the classroom book corner and evaluate the impact of the area she created. During

$\rightarrow$

her school experience Charlotte had worked with a Year 1 class. When she arrived the book corner was well organised but there was no particular display to promote reading across the curriculum. Charlotte took some photographs as a record of her starting point. After discussion with her class teacher she decided to base her book corner around the theme of picture books by Martin Waddell. The book corner continued to house books by a range of authors and included fiction, non-fiction and poetry but Charlotte created a focus display on her chosen author to link in with the class's current literacy focus on stories with predictable and patterned language. The school had a good range of books by Martin Waddell including *Farmer Duck, Pig in the Pond, Once there were Giants, Owl Babies, Snow Bears* and *Can't You Sleep Little Bear?* The school had a story sack to support the reading of Owl Babies and Charlotte was able to obtain a poster of Pig in the Pond from the local children's bookshop. During an art lesson the children used pastels to create their own versions of Neligen's pig making a big splash in the pond. Charlotte developed an engaging display using the children's pictures and depicting the onomatopoeic word 'splash' in different formats. To promote reading across the curriculum Charlotte also displayed non-fiction books about farms and farmyard animals and the poetry collection Cock a Doodle Doo: Farmyard Poems. Charlotte and the class teacher placed some soft toys of farm animals in the area and another teacher offered the loan of some cushions that depicted farm animals. Several of the children then brought in animal toys from home to add to the area. In her evaluation Charlotte was able to identify the children's increased motivation and confidence in using the book corner and their closer knowledge of the books in the collection after they had contributed to its development.

Charlotte's own first class are Year 2 and she is keen to build on her student project by involving the children in the organisation and display of the book area. Charlotte decides that she may well develop an author theme later during her first year but that she will start with something more generic as a way of finding out about the children's reading habits. Each child is asked to create a 'My favourite book' mini-poster which will be displayed in the area. Each child's poster will include a photograph of themselves and, where possible, the favourite book will also be on display. Charlotte is keen to encourage the children to recognise that their personal choice can be fiction, non-fiction or poetry and that all readers are different with their own tastes and preferences. Charlotte creates a mini-poster of The Owl who was Afraid of the Dark by Jill Tomlinson, which was her own favourite book from when she was six. She also includes a photograph of herself at about that age. Charlotte and the class very quickly make the reading corner look more inviting and personal to them. Charlotte knows that in the longer term she will need to decide on the best way to organise the books, which might again draw on the children's contribution. She will also need to evolve a time efficient way of keeping the book corner lively and inviting.

Links to the National Curriculum

Pupils' interest and pleasure in reading is developed as they learn to read independently.

The range should include print and electronic texts including: stories with predictable language, poetry from a range of cultures and reference texts.

Like Charlotte you will probably have a book corner or reading area to organise for your first class. The format for this may be partly dependent on the age of your class. Early years and Key Stage 1 classes tend to have a designated 'area'. In Key Stage 2 this isn't always the case, although you might feel that it should be, but there will almost certainly be a collection of books to be organised and promoted within the physical space available. If you are very fortunate you might be allocated a budget to add to the collection of books in your classroom. You will certainly need to ascertain what is there, whether or not all the material is appropriate and where the resourcing gaps might be.

Activity

Resourcing your book corner – who to consider

Select an age group that particularly interests you. This could be the year group for your next school experience or, if you are near the end of your programme, you may already know the age of your first class. Reflect on the considerations that you will need to make to ensure there is a wide and appropriate range of reading material for all the children in the class. Remember that your classroom collection should include fiction, non-fiction and poetry. There may also be plays, comics and children's newspapers, electronic texts and other non-book materials. Books written by the children themselves are often some of the most popular books in a classroom collection. A few pointers have been given to get you started on a review of the books in your classroom (see page 169).

Links to the National Curriculum

Teachers should set high expectations and provide opportunities for all children to achieve.

Children should experience a range of literature including fiction, non-fiction and non-literary texts.

The range should include print and electronic texts including: modern fiction, long established children's authors, modern and classic poetry, play scripts, myths, legends and traditional stories, diaries, biographies and autobiographies, newspapers, magazines and texts drawn from a range of cultures and traditions.

Range and variety of material and awareness of children in your class.	Points to consider when auditing or adding to the books in your classroom. List notes and further questions.
Topics across the curriculum that will be covered during the school year	*Which topics will be covered in science, history, geography, religious education, art and design, design technology? Does the book collection include fiction and non-fiction books that link to these topics?* *Is it possible to enhance the collection by drawing on the school library collection at certain times of the year? Does the local authority library have a loaning service for schools?*
Books that offer a positive representation of our multicultural society	*Which books in the collection offer children a positive and accurate 'window on the world'? Are there also books which offer ALL children a 'mirror' to learn more about themselves?*
Books that highlight our personal lives or relate to PSHE and citizenship	*Does the collection include books which explore families and friendships? Do some of the books reflect children's future lives as active, global citizens? Are there books which deal with very sensitive issues such as bereavement? How will you present these books? Which other personal, social and citizenship themes might you want to see reflected in the book collection?*
Boys	*What has research highlighted for you about the pattern of many boys' reading? How will this inform your review of the books available? How will you develop boys' interests and draw on research evidence without perpetuating stereotypes?*
Girls	*Are we in danger of neglecting the reading needs of girls? What considerations will you make in reviewing the books available? Again you will need to consider how you will develop girls' reading and at the same time avoid the perpetuation of stereotypes.*
Children for whom English is an additional language	*How many children in your class have English as an additional language? What is their first language? What is their stage of English proficiency? How will you ensure books written in English are both language and age appropriate? Will bilingual language texts also be available?*
More able readers	*Does the range include books that will offer a broad reading experience? Are the books still age appropriate?*
Less advanced readers	*What do you know about the qualities of books that support both decoding and meaning making? Are there a good range of books like this available? Are they age appropriate?*
Non book materials	*Does the classroom collection include comics, newspapers, audio books and electronic texts?*
Additional reviews you would wish to undertake in relation to the class collection?	
A final and very important question	*How good is your personal knowledge of the books you have reviewed? Your ability to promote books to the children will be dependent, not only on your knowledge of the specific titles, but also of other books by the same authors and books on similar themes that the children might enjoy. Some resources for keeping up to date with children's books are given at the end of this chapter.*
Use your notes above to evaluate the quality and overall range and variety of books available in your classroom. Your notes will also be a useful basis if you feel you need to ask for additional resources or if you have been given a budget to spend.	

The management and organisation of your classroom to promote children's use of English and the provision of a stimulating and appropriate reading area or book corner are essential. These are likely to be very tangible tasks in your early days and weeks as a class teacher. It will be important also to consider the ethos you aim to establish. The ethos is the culture and philosophy of your classroom. Whilst you could take photographs of your classroom displays and your book collection, you might think of the ethos as that which cannot be photographed but which would be evident to a visitor spending time in your classroom. Research has identified different dimensions of this ethos and why it is so important in the promotion of speaking, listening, reading and writing across the curriculum.

Research Focus

Chambers (1985) used the expression 'book talk' to emphasise the importance of children and teachers talking about books as a central dimension of the reading environment. Similarly Barrs and Thomas (1991) stressed that 'enthusiasm for books is caught not taught.' Fox (1992) asserted that a positive literacy environment involves children as speakers and listeners who create and tell their own stories. Fox also identified that the literacy environment is not just the physical 'props' of the classroom but a community. The most influential figure within this community is the teacher because the teacher can influence children's reading attitudes both directly and by facilitating the children to influence each other.

In 2008 Gamble and Yates cited the importance of teacher knowledge about children's literature. This has also been emphasised in the United Kingdom Literacy Association (UKLA) 'Teachers as Readers' project which has identified the importance of teachers' subject knowledge of children's literature and the positive influence of teachers who share their own reading habits and preferences as active reading role models (Cremin et al., 2008). As teachers involved in the project developed their knowledge of children's literature and became more aware of their own reading lives, they were able to create a stronger sense of a reading community which had a very positive influence on children's attitudes. Improvements in attitude and attainment have also been identified in The Power of Reading Project initiated by the Centre for Language in Primary Education (CLPE). Once again the emphasis is on teacher knowledge of literature and a focus on reading for pleasure.

Reading for pleasure and reading motivation are important not least because children who enjoy reading are likely to read more often and for longer than those who do not. Cunningham and Stanovich (1998) have demonstrated links between the amount of time spent reading and children's attainment. The benefits of regular reading are also highlighted by The Progress in International Reading Literacy Study (PIRLS) which has indicated that regular reading may be more

→

advantageous than having educated parents. The benefits of regular reading will be evident across the curriculum. PIRLS has also presented worrying evidence that children in England read less often for pleasure than children in other countries and that they have a more negative attitude to reading. This has inevitably, and quite rightly, prompted questions about the possible reasons for some children's failure to find enjoyment in reading. Any educational practices which leave children feeling negative about reading must be of concern to teachers and Pennac (2006) has argued for the 'rights of the reader.' Pennac's proposed rights include the right to read anything, the right not to finish a book and the right to reread. The significance of the texts themselves was stressed by Meek (1988) and Bearne (2003) has highlighted the need in the twenty-first century to recognise the diversity of multi-modal texts.

If you are passionate about reading yourself you will want to motivate the children in your class to become passionate readers. The research evidence tells you that this is also likely to have a positive impact on their academic success across the curriculum. A very powerful way to promote reading and to immerse children in the world of literature is to ensure that you make time to read aloud to your class every day. In Early Years and Key Stage 1 this is likely to include stories that can be read in one sitting but older children will enjoy sustaining a story over several days. Reading aloud demonstrates how the black marks on the page are brought alive and given meaning. It also has the potential to introduce a wide range of literature and to show children where their reading journey might be taking them. The range of texts you select will need to build on children's interests and can also reflect learning across the curriculum.

Some children will have a particular passion for reading or will enjoy expressing themselves through writing. For such children opportunities to develop their interest beyond lesson time can be very fulfilling. Most primary schools will have sports, music and art clubs and many schools also recognise the value of promoting English through extra-curricular activities.

Case Study: Running a readers' and writers' club and a school bookshop

Nadia is in the third year of her four year undergraduate teaching programme. As part of an enhancement project she has arranged her own school placement to explore the role of the English subject leader. She is particularly interested in how English is promoted beyond the timetabled curriculum and will be completing a report and evaluation of her research. Nadia shadows Richard, a very experienced English coordinator. One particular initiative with which Nadia becomes involved is the readers' and writers' club. The club runs during two lunchtimes a week. On Tuesday lunchtimes the club is attended by children in Years 5 and 6 and on Thursday lunchtimes some of the Year 6 children, supported by Richard, host a club for children in Years 3 and 4. The particular project that Nadia observes and

→

supports is the creation of a school newspaper. The Year 5 and 6 children act as interviewers, journalists and then editors, to produce a newspaper to celebrate the school's centenary. The children first set out their plans for the content of the newspaper and then allocate roles and responsibilities. Some of the children research the school's history while others interview current and former members of the school community. The newspaper, when complete, is 'published' during a special week of centenary celebrations.

Richard has kept a journal of the club's activities during his time at the school and Nadia gathers many other good ideas for her future practice. These include: writing letters to the local council about an environmental issue that had concerned the children, shadowing one of the children's national book awards, poetry writing on a range of topics, reading circles to discuss new books and the writing of reviews for the local bookshop. Nadia is impressed with the potential of this extra-curricular club to enhance children's learning in and through English and the opportunities children experience through working with children beyond their usual class grouping.

Nadia also has chance to support Richard in running the school bookshop. This operates on a Friday afternoon after school which encourages parents to stay and browse with their children. The children collect stamps to build towards book purchases and the shop sessions encourage a lot of book talk through children sharing their favourite books and making recommendations to friends. Nadia gathers details of various organisations that can provide and support similar projects. Details are given at the end of the chapter.

Links to the National Curriculum

Schools are able to provide learning opportunities outside the National Curriculum to meet the needs of individuals or groups.

Pupils experience a variety of writing genres and write for a range of purposes, audiences and contexts.

Pupils recognise how people can improve their environment and how decisions about places and environments affect the future quality of people's lives.

Activities such as a readers' and writers' club can be very rewarding not only for the children but also for the teachers involved. As a student you will have needed to be aware of the roles of colleagues who coordinate different dimensions of school life and may at times have called on the support of teachers with specific curriculum responsibilities. When you become an NQT your first challenge will be to consolidate your role as a class teacher but you may already be thinking about your future career development and possible areas of responsibility that would interest you. It is not usual to take on a curriculum leadership role until at least your second year of teaching but, in small schools in particular, you may find there is an expectation that you contribute to curriculum development fairy early on in your career. You will be aware that English is a very large and important area of the curriculum for which to have responsibility but, if you have a particular interest in English, it is possible to begin to show your interest in small ways. You might be asked initially to shadow the school's English or literacy coordinator. Some schools have curriculum teams in order to share the responsibility and to capitalise on teamwork and the expertise of more than one person. You might be asked to join the team. You can find ways to demonstrate your interest in English long before becoming a post holder. Be enthusiastic but take care not to 'tread on toes'. Ask the English or literacy coordinator what you might be able to do to support him or her in the role.

To demonstrate your passion for English first and foremost you should be a good model of English teaching in your own classroom. This should be evident in the environment of the classroom and the enthusiasm of you and your class. There are also specific projects you might take on within and beyond your classroom. These could include: organising a competition related to speaking, listening, reading or writing; arranging for an author or storyteller to visit school; initiating a book and comic 'bring and swap' event; planning an event for World Book Day such as a book character dressing up competition; hosting a family quiz evening based on children's books; establishing a paired reading venture between your class and older or younger children; becoming involved in the management and organisation of the school library.

Activities such as those above are one way of promoting English beyond the subjects of the curriculum. They can also be an important factor in creating a positive ethos for language, literature and literacy across the school. To further this sense of whole school community, schools often hold focus weeks. In relation to English this might involve a book week, a poetry week or a writers' workshop, perhaps with a writer in residence. Focus weeks need to be planned so that their impact continues beyond the conclusion of the week's events but a week of intense activity can be a very positive way to bring the school community together to celebrate learning. Through a combination of daytime and after school activities it is often possible to involve parents and grandparents, preschool children and also former pupils who have moved on to secondary school. Participation in a school book week is one way, even as a student or NQT, that you can feel fully involved in the whole school community.

Case Study: Participating in a school book week

William and Sophie, first year undergraduate students, are on their first school experience in a two form entry junior school. It is the spring term and the school's annual book week is scheduled for the fifth week of the six week placement allowing William and Sophie to be involved, not only in the focus week, but in all the preparations. At the start of the placement William and Sophie participate in a staff meeting which gives some insight into the planning that has already taken

→

place. The theme for the week is 'Turning stories into books' and each class will be writing and producing their own books inspired by the work of a designated author. There will also be an opportunity to focus on non-fiction books linked to different areas of learning. The English coordinator, Heather, explains that the date for the book week had been confirmed in the school calendar at the end of the previous summer term and that she first began setting out an outline of the week's activities early in the school year. The visitor and whole school events were established in the plan first, culminating in a sharing of book week work on the Friday morning and a character dress parade on the Friday afternoon.

Heather explains that it is particularly important to start planning early if you hope to book a visiting children's author. The school has had some very successful author visits in the past but has decided this time to keep their costs down and to have several visitors during the week rather than one big author visit. The visitors will include a parent who illustrates books, a traditional book binder from a local crafts complex, a collector of antique books and a storyteller. The timetable has been constructed so that all the children will have chance to benefit from a storytelling session and to meet at least two of the other visitors.

A large number of parents have volunteered their skills, including reading to groups of children and running activity workshops sharing personal hobbies and skills inspired by a range of non-fiction books. The workshops have been organised in mixed age groups to give children chance to work in different settings. The aim is to promote a wide range of the school's non-fiction books and the workshops include: a variety of arts, crafts, design and model making, wild flower identification, cookery, local history, gardening and bird watching. The opportunity for parents to share their expertise proves to be very successful and adds to the sense of the school as a community. William leads some workshops to share his interest in orienteering and Sophie leads workshops in photography. On the Friday afternoon William makes the most of his height by appearing as the BFG and Sophie dresses as Varjak Paw. They feel very honoured to be asked to judge the character parade. There are book token prizes for the best dressed characters in each year group but all the children are praised for their costumes, most of which are home-made and demonstrate some very creative thinking.

William and Sophie thoroughly enjoy the experience. They have learned how valuable a focus week can be to bring a fresh impetus to learning and that a book week can be very cross-curricular. They have also recognised that planning a successful book week involves good team collaboration and a lot of planning and preparation.

Links to the National Curriculum

English

Pupils' interest and pleasure in reading is developed as they learn to read confidently and independently;

Pupils use reference materials for different purposes;

Pupils engage in a range of practical tasks that develop a range of techniques, skills, processes and knowledge; Design and technology.

Pupils use appropriate fieldwork techniques and instruments; Geography

Pupils collect visual and other information to help them develop their ideas; Art and design

Pupils understand the roles and purposes of artists, crafts people and designers; Art and design

Learning Outcomes Review

The chapter has explored the potential to use and learn about English beyond the context of the school curriculum. This has included a consideration of the management and organisation of the classroom and the daily routines of school life. The importance of children finding pleasure in reading, and the link to success across the whole curriculum, has been emphasised. The notion of a positive classroom ethos for literacy and the importance of promoting English across the whole school community have been highlighted. Case study examples have illustrated how you might contribute to English beyond your own classroom.

Self-assessment questions

1. Identify ten examples of how your classroom organisation can support children to use English for meaningful purposes. Your suggestions might include examples linked to subjects across the curriculum and examples related to day to day school life.
2. Suggest creative formats for children to review books to encourage 'book talk'.
3. Suggest examples to involve the whole school community in celebrating speaking, listening, reading and writing either during a focus week or throughout the school year.

Further Reading

Books for Keeps and Carousel: The Guide to Children's Books, are both excellent for keeping up to date with children's books.

http://booksforkeeps.co.uk/

http://www.carouselguide.co.uk/

Love Reading offers book suggestions for children, parents and teachers. http://www.lovereading4kids.co.uk/

Book Trust has themed booklists and also offers suggestions for running a school book week. http://www.booktrust.org.uk/

Scholastic provide visiting book fairs and resources and suggestions for running a school book club. http://www.scholastic.co.uk/

Centre for Literacy in Primary Education (CLPE) www.clpe.co.uk

United Kingdom Literacy Association (UKLA) www.ukla.org

World Book Day http://www.worldbookday.com/

References

Barrs, M. and Thomas, A. (1991) *The Reading Book*. UK: CLPE.

Bearne, E. (2003) In Styles, M. and Bearne, E. (eds) (2003) *Art, Narrative and Childhood*. Stoke on Trent: Trentham Books.

Chambers, A. (1985) *Book Talk: Occasional Writing on Literature and Children*. London: Bodley Head.

CLPE (2005–2012) *Power of Reading Project*. UK.

Cremin, T. et al. (2008) *Teachers as Readers: Building Communities of Readers*. United Kingdom Literacy Association.

Cunningham, A.E. and Stanovich, K.E. (1998) What reading does for the mind, *American Educator*, 22 (1 and 2): 8–15.

Fox C. (1992) in Harrison, C. and Coles, M. *Reading for Real Handbook*. Oxford: Routledge.

Gamble, N. and Yates, S. (2008) *Exploring Children's Literature*. (2nd edition). London: SAGE.

Meek, M. (1988) *How Texts Teach What Readers Learn*. Stroud, Gloucestershire: Thimble Press.

Pennac, D. (2006) *The Rights of the Reader*. London: Walker Books.

Tickell, C. (2011) *The Early Years: Foundations for life, health and learning*. An Independent Report on the Early Years Foundation Stage to Her Majesty's Government, DFE.

Appendix 1: Model answers to the self-assessment questions

Chapter 1

1. Answers will vary, but could consider adherence to single subject curricular, planning without consideration for this, lack of consideration of cross-curricular opportunities.

2. Responses to this will be entirely personal, but will include the reading of this question!

3. Answers will include acknowledgement of tone, pace, content and language relevant to the audience and purpose.

Chapter 2

1. Chapter 2 should have helped you to think about the many ways that children learn through language. Answers will vary but you might have considered setting up collaborative contexts for children to investigate a mathematical problem, to explore historical sources such as artefacts or paintings in history or to evaluate a performance in dance or gymnastics in physical education. Opportunities for children to use English and to apply what they have learned about speaking, listening, reading and writing are apparent in all areas of the curriculum. You might have reflected on how children can develop and communicate ideas in design and technology or to present scientific data in an appropriate and systematic manner in science. Children might use their reading skills to interpret historical documents or geographical stories and information texts.

2. You are probably very conscious that children learn about the phonemic patterns of English and explore word choice and sentence structures in their own and others' writing. You should now also be aware that learning about language has a much broader potential than learning about language as a system, important though that knowledge is for children's competence. Other dimensions you have considered might include learning about how language has changed over time and how it continues to change and exploring the many forms of language variety within and between languages and for different audiences, contexts and purposes. Cross-curricular potential provides very meaningful contexts for this exploration.

3. You might have identified planning approaches in which language exploration is a major thread running through another subject or just a focused language lesson that links to other curriculum work. You should also have identified that valuable reflection on language can occur incidentally and that this can enhance children's concept development in other areas of learning.

4. Answers will vary but you might have considered how information and communication technology can support children to plan, draft, review and edit their writing. You might have recognised that children can use language to evaluate compositions and performance in music and that musical terminology often provides interesting word families to explore (e.g. choir, choral, chorus). Learning a foreign language provides a real and meaningful context to explore language variety and to notice cognates, words in different languages which have similar meanings and origins (e.g. airport English, aéroport French, aeropuerto Spanish, aeroporto Italian).

Chapter 3

1. Answers will vary. The starting points you choose are largely personal. For example, you could start from a book that you know well or a book that the children have selected and plan the learning from that or you could find books related to the topic or learning you wish to cover in your lessons. One important consideration is relevance; you need to ensure that the literature is appropriate and the cross-curricular learning is worthwhile.

2. Answers will vary. These might include; exploration of contentious issues in a safe and supported context, enhancement of children's understanding of their world, making relevant links between subjects to develop learning, increasing accessibility of learning, widening children's experience of literature, encouraging positive attitudes to reading.

3. The links you suggest will be your own ideas as will the adaptations or improvements you are able to make.

4. The books you select will be personal choices and there is a multitude of possibilities. It may be that you have experienced cross-curricular learning through literature yourself or have seen it successfully implemented in schools.

5. The activity previously suggested in this chapter will have acquainted you with children's libraries. The bookshops you visit will depend on your locality. You may be lucky enough to have access to an independent children's bookshop which is a tremendous resource to be utilised. If not, high street chains offer some variety and many supermarkets also stock children's books. In addition, make use of the internet as this provides an extensive selection of texts.

Chapter 4

1. Reference books on a range of topics, magazines, newspapers, atlases, different types of dictionaries (definition, spelling, etymological, bilingual, specialised, e.g. A–Z of World Religions), thesauri, catalogues, instruction manuals, recipes and comics should be made available to children. Children should also access online non-fiction texts.

2. Children will need to understand the structural and language features of different text types and be able to use them accurately in their independent writing. They should have a good

understanding of the audience and purpose of their factual writing and the need to use particular subject-specific vocabulary. They should also recognise that some writing will incorporate features from a number of different text types.

Chapter 5

1. Other adults provide alternative models of English for EAL pupils. They also provide classroom support for academic tasks like writing, consolidating and rehearsing language before a lesson. Bilingual adults can also provide support in the pupils' home language. Parental support can assist pupils in addressing their cultural heritage and act as a useful and relevant bridge between home and school literacy practices.

2. Classrooms should be print rich environments that enable pupils to access the English necessary to fulfil their daily tasks independently. They should also reflect the range of cultures present in the classroom in a way that moves beyond tokenism. In order to do this classroom display needs to be updated and reflective of current classroom projects that integrate and contextualise the curriculum and reflect the integral place of language.

3. A range of answers is possible depending on the level of English learning in the EAL pupils. They may include:
   - Grouping, a ratio of one EAL speaker to two native English speakers is useful
   - Providing dual language dictionaries
   - Maximising visual cues for learning
   - Pre-teaching of key concepts and language via the learning support assistant
   - Using story to activate knowledge of necessary language and concepts in real life contexts
   - Providing a visual timetable of the daily and weekly curriculum
   - Providing amanuensis
   - Providing 'survival language' cards for new arrivals with limited English
   - Cross-curricular lesson planning that isolates the key concepts and language necessary to access the topic and provides opportunities to recall and rehearse these in each lesson
   - Using a language survey
   - Effective questioning
   - Modelling

Chapter 6

1. Reasons for teaching thinking skills include the following.
   - More able to take responsibility for their own learning and become more independent learners.
   - Provides a structure to support children's thinking.
   - Have a sense of involvement in their learning and a clear sense of context and purpose.

- Learn from each other.
- Develop the skills to work more successfully in group and class situations.
- Work in an environment that has a clear ethos and values.
- Have time to reflect.
- Encourages children to sustain interest in a task.
- Learn to talk with more confidence.
- Learn to listen more carefully.
- Learn to respect others and value their opinions.
- They can be applied across the curriculum.

2. This is an example of a cross-curricular activity which will support children's development of critical, creative and co-operative thinking. The children in this Year 4 class were finding it difficult to develop the skills necessary to listen to each other's contributions in class discussions. This activity was planned to support the children's research and establish appropriate rules for the class for speaking and listening. Firstly the children were asked to use their critical thinking by designing a questionnaire to ask different year groups what their class rules were. The class were then divided into groups and it was arranged for the groups to observe how speaking and listening was organised in different classes. The children's co-operative thinking skills were then used as each group discussed the results of their research and suggested a list of rules for supporting speaking and listening. Each group was then asked to use their creative thinking to discuss additional rules or other organisational features that would support class speaking and listening. The final part of the activity involved the three aspects of thinking as the children worked together to provide a list of rules for their class.

Chapter 7

1. • Meet parents or carers before the child joins the class.

- Gather data from previous school, including medical data.
- Provide parents with information about the school day.
- Explain to parents about collection and assembly points at the beginning and end of each school day.
- Discuss lunchtime and homework arrangements.
- Show the family the classroom.

2. The key differences in reporting assessment data relate to an understanding of how the data will be interpreted by the different audiences for whom it is prepared. For example, data for parents will only relate to their own child. It will not contain excessive amounts of incomprehensible detail or jargon. It will be accompanied by practical details of how the parent can help their child to progress.

3. Schools may have a Literacy or English Policy that addresses the distinct modes of language and literacy development:

- Speaking and Listening
- Reading
- Writing
- Spelling
- Handwriting/Presentation

Chapter 8

1. Primary English teachers should read peer reviewed journals and professional journals in order to keep abreast of new research findings and to develop new teaching and learning ideas for the classroom. It also provides a balance to governmental publications and statutory directives.

2. The key features of action research listed in this chapter are:
   - Formulating a research question
   - Preliminary discussion with colleagues
   - Literature review
   - Modify initial question
   - Select research procedures
   - Select data analysis procedures
   - Carry out project
   - Interpretation of the data and dissemination of findings

3. Effective tips for formulating effective research questions in teaching and learning include:
   - Read the latest outputs from national and international organisations such as Ofsted, the National Literacy Trust and the International Reading Association
   - Take base line and observational data
   - Phrase the question as a hypothesis
   - Decide on the form or forms of analysis before the question can assist in clarifying its limitations
   - Rewrite the question after the literature review

4. Cross-curricular primary English themes include key aspects of the four modes of English. These include:
   - Reading motivation
   - Shared reading and writing
   - Implicit and explicit use of language, including grammar
   - Research skills

- Note taking
- Developing a purpose and audience for written and spoken English
- Presentation skills

Chapter 9

1. Answers will vary. You may have considered, for example, the interdependent world in which children live, the importance of being globally responsible, supporting children to understand events in the world, helping children to become aware of and respectful of others.

2. The case studies illustrate several different ways you could do this and you may have suggested some of your own. You could, for example, suggest ways drawn from examples of cross-curricular learning in other chapters of this book.

3. Answers will vary, but might include the exploration of relevant children's books, internet research, and debate and discussion between children.

4. Again, answers will vary but might include the case studies above or other examples you have personally experienced.

5. You might consider using children's literature, creating opportunities for discussion, or using reference materials to research.

6. Answers will vary and may include examples from your own teaching or indeed your own learning.

Chapter 10

1. Examples of how your classroom organisation can support children to use English for meaningful purposes. Your suggestions might include the following.

   - A classroom noticeboard for the use of the teacher, children and parents;
   - Cloakroom labels and signposting;
   - Timetable for the week showing the days that specific kit and equipment need to be brought to school;
   - Daily timetable, perhaps using changeable cards that can be placed in the appropriate order for that day;
   - A date board;
   - A weather board;
   - Labelling of curriculum resources to support children's independence in managing their learning;
   - Instructions for how to care for, clear up and put away materials used in art and design or design and technology;

- A display of reminders about how to be a good response partner for a friend's writing;
- A word wall for the current focus in English;
- A vocabulary display for the current focus in a particular subject.

2. Suggest creative formats for children to review books to encourage 'book talk'.
   - Collect, or make, related objects and display them with the book;
   - Draw a map of a journey made in the book;
   - Use circle time, or hold a class debate, to discuss issues raised by a text;
   - Write a CV for a favourite character;
   - Produce a leaflet to advertise the book;
   - Compile a collection of favourite quotes from the book;
   - Write a key event from the story as a newspaper report or summarise as a news headline;
   - Design a costume suitable for one of the characters;
   - Hold a balloon debate: in role as authors, or characters, children must justify their place in a sinking balloon;
   - Set up a computer database for children to log brief reviews.

3. Suggest examples to involve the whole school community in celebrating speaking, listening, reading and writing either during a focus week or throughout the school year.
   - Invite parents who speak a language other than English to share books in their first language and to explain something about the writing system if it is very different to English;
   - Initiate a search for the oldest book or the largest and smallest books that can be found in the school community and create a display;
   - Invite parents, children and teachers to write a poem on a chosen theme;
   - Invite parents and children to attend an opening ceremony for a new school bookshop or following a revamp of the school library and follow it with a children's book quiz;
   - Invite parents to a children's poetry recital;
   - Make a display of teachers' favourite books from when they were at primary school or ask parents to contribute a review of their favourite childhood books for classroom display;
   - Invite parents, children and former pupils to attend an author evening.

Appendix 2: Language books

Ayto, J. and Simpson, J. (2010) *The Oxford Dictionary of Modern Slang*. Oxford: Oxford University Press.

Beal, G. (2000) *Word Origins (Fun with English)*. London: Kingfisher Books.

Beal, G. and Chatterton, M. (1993) *The Kingfisher First Thesaurus*. London: Kingfisher Books.

Beal, G. and Stevenson, P. (1992) *Kingfisher Book of Words*. London: Kingfisher Books.

British Library Sound Archive http://sounds.bl.uk/Accents-and-dialects and http://www.bl.uk/learning/langlit/sounds/index.html

Bryson, B. (1990) *Mother Tongue: The English Language*. London: Penguin Books.

Crystal, D. (2007) *How Language Works*. London: Penguin Books.

Dalby, A. (2006) *Dictionary of languages: the definitive reference to more than 400 languages*. London: A & C Black Publishers Ltd.

Deary, T. (1996) *Horrible Histories: Wicked Words*. London: Scholastic Children's Books.

Dent, S. (2011) *How to Talk Like a Local: From Cockney to Geordie*. Croydon: Arrow Books.

Elmes, S. (2006) *Talking for Britain: A Journey through the Voices of a Nation*. London: Penguin Books.

Foyle, C. (2007) *Foyle's Philavery: A Treasury of Unusual Words*. St Ives: Chambers.

Foyle, C. (2007) *Foyle's Further Philavery: A Cornucopia of Lexical Delights*. St Ives: Chambers.

Gulland, D.M. and Hinds-Howell, D. (1994) *The Penguin Dictionary of English Idioms*. London: Penguin Books.

Jack, A. (2006) *Red Herrings and White Elephants: The Origins of the Phrases We Use Every Day*. London: Metro Publishing Ltd.

Jack, A. (2006) *Shaggy Dogs and Black Sheep: The Origins of Even More Phrases We Use Every Day*. London: Penguin Books.

Kacirk, J. (1999) *Forgotten English*. USA, Quill: William Morrow.

Mills, A.D. (2011) *A Dictionary of British Place Names*. Oxford: Oxford University Press.

Robinson, J. (2010) *CD Voices of The UK: Accents and Dialects of English*. British Library.

Room, A. (2000) *Cassell's Foreign Words and Phrases*. London: Cassell.

Speake, J. (1999) *Dictionary of Idioms*. Oxford: Oxford University Press.

Trask, R.L. (2003) *Language: The Basics*. London: Routledge.

Wilson, A. (2005) *Language Knowledge for Primary Teachers*. London: David Fulton.

Appendix 3: Children's literature books

Ahlberg, J. and Ahlberg, A. (1999) *Jeremiah in the Dark Woods*. London: Puffin.

Angelou, M. (1993) *Life Doesn't Frighten Me*. New York: Stewart, Tabori & Chang.

Carle, E. (1969) *The Very Hungry Caterpillar*. London: Puffin.

Currey, A. (2000) *Cock a Doodle Doo: Farmyard Poems*. Place: Macmillan.

Dahl, R. (1982) *The BFG*. London: Puffin.

Demi (1997) *One Grain of Rice*. New York: Scholastic.

Dunn, J. and Bate, H. (2008) *ABC UK*. London: Frances Lincoln.

Foreman, M. (1972) *Dinosaurs and all that Rubbish*. London: Puffin Books.

Fromenthal, J. and Jolivet, J. (2006) *365 Penguins*. Paris: Abrams Inc.

Hastings, S. (2005) *The Children's Illustrated Bible*. London: Dorling Kindersley.

Hill, E. (1980) *Where's Spot?* London: Picture Puffin.

Hooper, M. (2007) *At the House of the Magician*. London: Bloomsbury.

Hughes, S. (1981) *Alfie*. London: Red Fox.

Inkpen, M. (1991) *Kipper*. Place: Hodder Children's Books.

McKee, D. (1989) *Elmer*. Place: Anderson Press Ltd.

Pullman, P. (1995) *The Firework Maker's Daughter*. New York: Doubleday.

Said, S.F. (2004) *Varjak Paw*. London: Corgi.

Smith, D. and Armstrong, S. (2003) *If the World Were a Village*. London: A & C Black.

Tomlinson, J. (1968) *The Owl Who Was Afraid of the Dark*. Place: Publisher.

Waddell, M. and Barton, J. (1992) *The Pig in the Pond*. London: Walker.

Waddell, M. and Benson, P. (1992) *Owl Babies*. London: Walker.

Waddell, M. and Firth, B. (1992) *Can't You Sleep Little Bear?* London: Walker.

Waddell, M. and Fox-Davies, S. (2004) *Snow Bears*. London: Walker.

Waddell, M. and Oxenbury, H. (1992) *Farmer Duck*. London: Walker.

Index